QUILTS

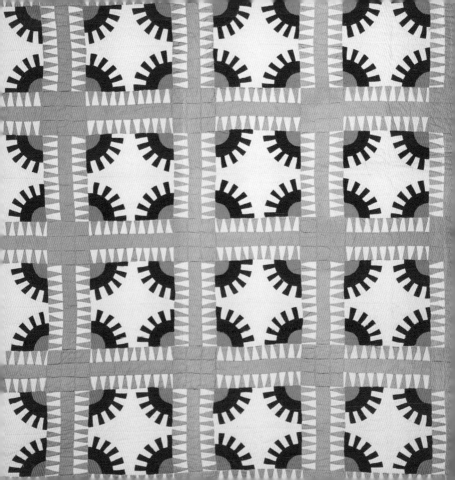

QUILTS

A Beautiful History

Zaro Weil

MQP

Published by MQ Publications Ltd
12 The Ivories, 6–8 Northanmpton Street,
London, N1 2HY
Tel: +44 (0) 20 7359 2244
Fax: +44 (0) 20 7359 1616
email: mail@mqpublications.com
www.mqpublications.com

ISBN: 1-84072-973-2

1 3 5 7 9 0 8 6 4 2

Printed and bound in China

CONTENTS

Introduction

Every individual is part and parcel of a great picture of society in which he lives and acts, and his life cannot be painted without reproducing the picture of the world he lived in.

Harriet Beecher Stowe, *Old Town Folks*, 1869

Quilts have been a high-spirited artistic expression of American women over the past two hundred years. Today, quilts are being reappraised by historians, art critics, and a growing international public as a unique and valuable legacy of American folk art. For the first time, the extraordinary creativity of generations of American women is gaining recognition. Quilts are no longer stored away in cupboards and trunks. Happily they are finding their way back into our lives, and enriching our homes. Many can also be found on the walls of some of the most important galleries and museums in the world. Quilts have come to represent a remarkable design tradition which has developed in the United States, since colonial times.

Right: Detail of *Ohio Rose* appliqué, American, 1930.

1 Colonial America

They fell upon their knees and blessed the God of heaven, who had brought them over the vast and furious ocean, and delivered them from all the perils and miseries thereof, againe to set their feete on the firme and stable earth, their proper elemente...they had no friends to welcome them, nor inns...no houses or much less townes to repaire too, to seek for succoure...

These were the words of Governor William Bradford, who witnessed and reported the landing of the Mayflower passengers. The early settlers who came to the shores of the New World were, within a few short years, caught up in the routine of everyday life—the crop season, maintaining the house and family, and basic survival. From the first landings at Jamestown in 1607, and Plymouth in 1620, America was dominated by scarcity and small-scale production. Life was regulated by the weather and seasons, and most families were tied to the local agricultural calendar. Yet after only 150 years, this uncivil land had prospered enough to emerge as a new civilization, and by 1750 the colonists came to be greatly affected by much larger events and ideas.

Religious attitudes, political uprisings, economic growth, cultural trends and the quality of domestic life were all critical factors in shaping the beliefs and concerns of successive generations. The women who created the unique legacy of the American quilt, from those living in East Coast mansions to those in frontier log cabins, expressed in their needlework a social history which reflected the rapidly changing character of American life.

In pre-Revolutionary America conditions were generally unfavorable for quiltmaking. Houses were small, cramped, and dirty. Imported material was scarce and expensive and homespun fabric was mostly used for other household items rather than quilted bedcovers. In addition, the commercial manufacture of cloth was strictly prohibited, although fabric, flax, seed, and sheep were smuggled into the country by various shippers, despite severe penalties.

For ordinary families fabrics were scarce and were used, reused, saved, and salvaged. Homespun fabric was painstakingly worked on the spinning wheel and loom by Colonial wives and daughters. This was a primary domestic task requiring a high level of skill.

Homemade dyes were also difficult to produce, and before the availability of dye books in the nineteenth century the art of coloring was nearly as important as clothmaking. Roots, berries, leaves, nuts, and barks were continually gathered for dye making and homemade recipes carefully guarded or exchanged.

In these conditions there was neither the time, the space, nor the money for most women even to consider making a beautiful quilt. Quilts made during this period were plain, rough affairs used until they simply fell apart or were recycled as linings for other bedcovers.

The New Middle Classes

The Revolutionary period of the 1770s saw the beginnings of small-scale manufacturing, with the war itself creating opportunities for expansion. One of the most important new industries, along with iron manufacturing, pottery, and glassworks, was textile manufacturing, particularly cotton, which was to play a substantial role in the development of the American quilt.

During the second half of the eighteenth century, the creation of leisure time, the abundance of imported materials, and a new social emphasis on domesticity made quilting widely popular. Women

Right: *Princess Feather*, American, nineteenth century, 76 x 74 in. (193 x 188 cm). This quilt has stuffed trapunto quilting in both the vine border and center blocks.

lavished more time creating elaborate pieced and appliquéd quilts. They were strongly influenced by the styles and methods of England, where the ability to sew and do fine needlework was a feminine priority. Newly established American Dame Schools and Young Ladies' Schools—types of finishing school for the middle classes—gave needlework prominence as a paramount accomplishment and a testimony to good breeding. Girls were often taught to sew from the age of three, and by the time they were five they had probably made their own four- or nine-patch quilt. Boys were also taught how to sew and cut patterns.

Certain social conventions governing quilting were established early on. The piecing and appliqué work that decorated the top came to be the work of a single maker, while the quilting, a separate step, might have been done either by the woman who pieced the top, by a professional quilter, or jointly by a group of friends.

English Traditions and American Borrowings

Because there are few known eighteenth century quilts surviving in America, knowledge of English influences is somewhat clouded. It is, however, known that the earlier sixteenth- and seventeenth-century English traditions of quilted wholecloth bedcoverings, block-patterned piecework quilts, and appliqué and pieced central medallion style quilts were popular in mid-eighteenth century England.

Many of the wholecloth quilts which are recorded or preserved are commonly called linsey-woolsey after Lindsey in Suffolk, England, where they originated. These quilts were very much the household staple and were made of a linen warp and a wool weft, creating a rather stiff, heavy fabric. They were stuffed with unbleached wool and finely quilted with loosely spun linen thread in fanciful arabesque and scroll designs. Brilliant shades of indigo blue, red, and brown from homemade dye vats created admirable colors on otherwise bulky utilitarian items.

After 1750 much more elegant wholecloth or pieced quilts were made from expensive fabric printed in the traditional hand-blocked method or with engraved copperplates. These would have been in either the popular pastoral style or the French-inspired *toile de Jouy* materials which depicted lavish historical or mythological scenes.

One of the most fashionable textile designs of seventeenth- to mid-nineteenth-century Europe was the Indo-European flowering tree motif. Large hand-painted or block-printed cotton panels known as palampores were produced to order in India for a European market. The introduction of such gaily colored cottons revolutionized the English textile trade in woolen and linen manufacture. Their cheapness and color took the public fancy. Women, who had previously dressed in woolen cloth, began to wear calico and printed linen. These painted and glazed colorfast Indian chintzes featured outsize flowers, exotic birds, trees, and colorful leaves and vines.

Despite years of bans on chintzes in Europe they were still affordable to society, and the highly valued leftovers came to be ingeniously stitched into bedcovers and counterpanes.

Figurative portions of the chintz—the birds, flowers, leaves or animals—were often cut out and then stitched directly onto a fine white wholecloth background, the overall pattern perhaps inspired by the popular Tree of Life motif. This appliqué style was known as *broderie perse*, or Persian embroidery, and may have been developed as a quick way to achieve the look of stylish embroidery or crewel work. The *broderie perse* style actually created a new design entirely out of pictorial patches.

By the mid-eighteenth century there were three distinct English needlework traditions which had found their way to American shores.

First there were the appliqué covers—often made to cover daybeds in English country houses—with their characteristic spaciousness of design, large central flower panels (often cut from bold chintzes), or specially printed medallion centers. Then there were the pieced patchworks composed entirely of stitched shapes—hexagons, diamonds, squares, and rectangles, sometimes with a central medallion panel. Finally, there was the quilted wholecloth covering, as elaborate or simple as time and circumstance dictated.

The Revolutionary Period

Changes in Religion

After the Revolution, the widespread expansion of trade presented many families with new economic and social opportunities. The transition had begun from the medieval guild outlook, which had dominated American Colonial life for nearly 200 years, to a new commercial mentality. The restrictive doctrines of the church, which frowned upon material acquisitions, lost ground in the emerging Republic. In the 1790s a religious revival movement called The Great Awakening emerged as a counter-offensive to austere Calvinist thinking, offering a more generous and loving picture of God.

This awakening was important in the story of quilting because it transferred the responsibility for moral and religious education directly from clergymen to women in the home. Women were called upon to establish a domestic environment where suitable training would be offered to America's future citizens. Thus began a cult of domesticity, which in the early years of the nineteenth century encouraged the creation of a well-ordered and comfortable domestic setting.

This new cult of domesticity was the main reason for the widespread development of needlework and quilting as occupations thought suitable for women. By 1800 it was considered necessary and proper for a young lady not only to acquire a thorough knowledge of needlework, but also to gain an insight into a science, such as botany, in order to become a better homemaker, companion, and conversationalist.

Right: This engraving from Frank B. Goodrich's *The Tribute Book*, shows a quilting party at work.

2 A New Democracy

In 1800, some twenty-four years after the end of the Revolution, the
area of America had doubled to 18 million square miles. The pace of
westward expansion accelerated, and by 1820 more than 2.2 million
people had settled in the Missouri Valley. A rapidly developing
transportation system of waterways and roads, itinerant peddlers,
religious circuit riders, medicine shows, and social gatherings
facilitated the exchange of information and ideas. Sewing bees, get-
togethers, agricultural fairs, ladies' fairs, and church bazaars were
common events. Also, greater literacy among both women and men,
especially in the New England area, allowed a wider scope for the
circulation of news and ideas. By 1800 more than 180 newspapers
were being published throughout the states, as well as important
broadsides, magazines and books, and the almanacs of the early 1800s
carried quilt patterns for the benefit of their female readers. These
factors strongly contributed to the spread of new quilting methods and
patterns which seemed to emerge at random, and yet simultaneously
across the growing nation.

Increasing Popularity of Quilting

After the Revolutionary War, and again after the War of 1812 against Britain, British merchants, anxious to make up the profits they had lost during the years of conflict, flooded the American market with manufactured goods. These included a great deal of fabric which was purchased by well-to-do families and used for furnishings, fine clothing, and quilts.

At the same time, new Republican policies dictated a fresh set of domestic and moral responsibilities for women which encouraged the role of quilting and needlework. Because few rural households were fully self-sufficient, it was customary for families both to barter with the local store (exchanging produce for nails, rum, or cloth etc.,) and to exchange goods and services with each other.

It became a broadly followed tradition for neighborhoods to interact through mutual visiting and frolics. Most important of these gatherings were the house- and barn-raisings, and the get-togethers—often composed of women only—for needlework and textile production, in particular the quilting bees.

Quilting also took on a wider social aspect and often involved the entire family. Everyone seemed to participate in the making of quilts, whole families were involved. Husbands and fiancés drew complex patterns on a quilt top or cut out templates from which patterns were cut. Grandmothers and children threaded needles and cut out patches, while mothers sewed pieces together and quilted the top. A quilt in some instances represented the creative efforts of an entire family.

Domestic Life

By 1830 there were significant contrasts between the houses of ordinary and well-off families. The small farmers and settlers venturing westward continued to recreate earlier conditions of domestic life. Log cabins were the primary housing unit. They were small, with peeling bark, and cracks that needed to be continually filled with mud. Indeed, worn-out quilts were often cut into strips and stuffed into the chinks in the walls.

Houses with more than one room would be separated into private and public space, with one room for working and the other, the parlor or chamber, for both sleeping and entertaining.

While most of the family might have slept under a woolen bedcover, perhaps patched or roughly quilted, the parlor was not considered well furnished unless it had a best bed, covered with an appropriately best bedcover or quilt. This may have given rise to the dual tradition of the plain and the fancy quilt: the former strictly utilitarian, the latter more decorative.

The New Pieced Block Quilt Style

While early quilts and coverlets made by the colonists were planned with consideration to the design as a whole, by the early 1800s more and more women were making individual blocks and then setting them together with strips or latticework, or with alternate white blocks. This new block technique allowed for more experimentation with traditional design elements. Squares and triangles were pieced together in innovative ways. Stars grew more elaborate and "sprouted serrated edges called feathers and grew to cover an entire top in the Star of Bethlehem design. Squares were organized into Irish Chains, and triangles into sawteeth. Circular patterns fractured into Mariner's Compasses and Sunflowers."[1]

Traditional appliqué designs in the central medallion tradition incorporating trees, flowers, leaves or vines became stylized into repeated patterns and were often encircled with elaborate borders. Something new was happening—more women were making quilts and these quilts looked different and were made differently from the early English quilts that came before.

Earlier researchers had expressed the view that this new design motif was probably more functional since at the time rooms were too small and fabric too expensive for a complete quilt to be worked on as a whole. Other accounts speculate that the new American spirit of growth and energy was translated into inventive quilt designs. While these suggestions all ring true, probably no one explanation accounts for the emergence of this new type of quilt.

There were also more technical factors which help to account for the development and popularity of the pieced block quilt, and one of the most crucial of these was the growth of a native textile industry.

Factories and Technology

The manufacture of cotton was America's first national industry. There were three major social effects of this early industrialization, the first being that demand for cotton turned the South into a one-crop economy and created a strong need for the cheap manpower necessary to raise such a labor-intensive crop. From the 1830s, slavery, which was already part of the Southern economy, grew at a record rate.

Secondly, because New England provided the appropriate physical conditions for industry—the small streams and swift-running rivers necessary for water power, and the coastal port facilities for transportation—it became the site for the nation's first industrial factories.

Finally, the abundance of cheap cotton prints made it possible for women of all social classes to take up quilting and ensured that the quilt would be made of cotton. This contributed to the democratization of the quilt.

It became a well-applauded feminine talent to make something beautiful out of a basket of old scraps, and the creation of a handmade quilt symbolized the apogee of womanhood. "The model Republican

woman was competent and confident. She could resist the vagaries of fashion; she was rational, benevolent, independent, self-reliant and dedicated to the service of civic virtue."[2] Her home was to be a warm, comforting and beautiful sanctuary away from the harsh world of trade and commercialism.

Thus, with the emphasis on the home and domestic skills, the handmade quilt came to be an important expression of national sentiment. As the American idea of democracy took root, and more families were able to acquire those material and cultural possessions which had for centuries been the domain of the rich, so the possession of a beautiful quilt became an accepted social aspiration.

Right: *Nine-patch* with *Flying Geese* border. 74 x 78 inches (188 x 198 cm). Imported English cottons were used to make this quilt, the earliest fabric on it dating from 1810. The design, with its squares and triangles, is typical of the many kinds of variations which were done during the period, while the rich madders and brown dyes, too, were popular colors at the time.

3 A Country in Transition

The mid-nineteenth century saw an increase in the popularity of quiltmaking. Women in all parts of the country, from the East coast through the Ohio and Mississippi valleys, to the plains and prairie states in the West, stitched a variety of new types of quilt. Quilting had come into its own.

This was due to specific technological and social developments; innovations such as the sewing machine, the improvement in roller printing for fabrics, and the development of dye chemistry continued to create better quality and more affordable material. At the same time, a revived spirit of Protestantism among the growing middle classes engendered an increasing network of women's sewing circles, often associated with the church, as well as benevolent and reform associations. Quilts were made to benefit worthy causes. This, coupled with a continuing tradition of bees, quiltings, get-togethers, fairs, and auctions, endowed quilts with new social meaning.

The functional, everyday, plain, patched, or tied quilt was reproduced in the conditions of scarcity which existed in frontier life. The lure of cheap land had drawn hundreds of wagon trains over the

Appalachian Mountains, thus constituting the first major wave of westward migration. Despite the isolated living conditions, records indicate that whenever possible, women also continued to get together to make more intricate quilts in these western territories. East of the Mississippi, however, the wealth created through the expansion of industry suggested new domestic possibilities. Homes became more elaborate and style in both furnishings and dress became an important consideration.

The majority of quilt patterns from this period reflect the changing domestic circumstances in the eastern states. New designs bearing imaginative and romantic-sounding names such as Philadelphia Pavement, Rose Wreath, and Princess Feather were created in colorful calico prints. However, some patterns related to the westward migration, and names such as Rocky Road to Kansas, Prairie Rose, and Indian Hatchet are equally evocative of the time. Innovation was highly valued and women spent many hours developing interpretations of popular designs.

Rapidly shifting patterns of geographical settlement during these years, coupled with more clearly defined social roles for men and women, drew women together both physically and emotionally.

"Most eighteenth- and nineteenth-century women lived in a world bounded by home, church, and the institution of visiting. Women helped each other with domestic chores and in times of sickness, sorrow, and trouble. Urban and town women were able to devote some of virtually every day to visits, teas or shopping trips with other women. Rural women developed a pattern of more extended visits that lasted weeks and sometimes months."[3] The strong ties between women within a community or family setting were often expressed in needlework. An Album or Friendship quilt, for example, where friends or family members each signed a block (either by embroidery or in indelible ink) to serve as a lasting memory, was often given as a memento to a family embarking on one of the overland trails.

The place of the quilt in the hearts and minds of the American people was thus confirmed in the middle of the last century. Despite the influence of English patterns, the quilt was now defined not by European traditions but rather by a new American spirit of growth and optimism.

The Album Quilt

An Album quilt is composed of a number of separately designed blocks incorporated into an overall quilt. The blocks themselves are often pictorial (although there are examples of pieced Album quilts), stitched in the appliqué technique and generally sewn by individual members of a family or group contributing jointly to the project. There is a special social significance in the Album or Friendship quilt in that it was made to commemorate or celebrate a particular social event which was important to its makers.

During the period 1840 to 1860 several types of Album quilt were popular. These included the Friendship quilts, Presentation quilts, Bride's Album quilts, and Autograph quilts. The remarkable Album quilt on page 188 highlights the life of an entire family and is beautifully composed, featuring a combination of highly stylized, folk-like and symbolic blocks.

The most well known of this type of quilt is undoubtedly the Baltimore Album quilt, prized for their unusual designs, exquisite craftsmanship, and striking beauty representing floral motifs, ships, churches, Baltimore monuments, and historic events. The designs in printed cottons were applied to individual cloth squares, measuring

16 to 18 inches (40.5 to 45.5 cm) which were then sewn together in series to form quilts. Since each quilt block is similar in spirit to the pages of an autograph album, these quilts were called Album quilts. The most distinguishing characteristic of the finest of these quilts, made in Baltimore between 1846 and 1852, is the imaginative manner in which the printed cottons were pieced together to suggest texture, shading, and contour.

Baltimore, Maryland, was the third largest seaport in the United States at the time. It was also the most important East Coast port used for exporting domestic cotton and for importing a wide variety of English, French, German, and Swiss fabrics and trims. Baltimore therefore amassed a great deal of wealth quite quickly, and these conditions gave rise to a leisured class of women who had sufficient time, money, and materials for the creation of such intricate needlework. In addition, professional needlewomen in Baltimore offered their services for a fee to both design and make the intricate blocks which would be stitched into Album and other types of quilts.

These included the Presentation quilt, which dates from the early 1800s and would have been made specifically to present to some well-known or respected figure as a suitable testimonial to his or her good deeds or work. Also, the Friendship quilt, examples of which—often with identifying names, dates, locations, and informative quotes and sayings—have provided a rich field for quilt scholars. These quilts, recalled from the usual realm of anonymity, have offered tangible evidence about the lives, relationships and concerns of particular women or groups of women at a particular time.

Pioneer Women

Many different ethnic groups played a role in the settlement of the West, including families from Germany and Scandinavia, while the very poor and dispossessed tended to settle in crowded urban centers. Traveling west in a Conestoga wagon with a yoke of eight oxen and supplies for a year took a considerable investment and those Americans who chose to undertake the arduous journey tended to be members of the middle classes.

It was considered a woman's duty not only to maintain the stability of the family unit in the new environment but also to provide a measure of refinement and domestic comfort to their crude homes. Rather than leave behind aspects of life that they regarded as civilized, women tried to recreate them on the prairie. Women would wallpaper

the sod walls with newsprint, crochet dainty covers for jars, make rag rugs for the floors, and hang curtains fashioned from newspapers, old sheets and even old petticoats.

The Homestead Act of 1862 required a settler to live on his claim for five years in order to perfect his title. This gave a character to farm life in the West which was very different for the old-world peasants who had lived in tightly knit villages. The average distance of half a mile between farms meant isolation and loneliness for many women, and in order to adjust to their new lives, pioneer women worked to establish their own schools and churches and created a network of associations which would provide female companionship. Both get-togethers to make a quilt, and the quilt itself served important social functions and provided women with a material means to soften

Left: Central to pioneer survival and success was the institution of the family, wherein each individual was forced by circumstance to work in a continuous and cohesive way. This carefully staged photograph displays the material possessions of a successful Nebraskan family. The wagon, horses, and outbuildings, as well as the striking quilt thrown over a hitching post, would all have been acquired over the years and are here proudly exhibited.

the harsh reality of the frontier. The popularity of the Album and Friendship quilts during this period testifies to the importance of personal bonds, both within families and among women.

Country and agricultural fairs, where quilts were prominently displayed and judged in contests, became an important feature of mid-nineteenth-century life. Initially, fairs tended to be livestock shows for the benefit of local farmers. Then, early in the nineteenth century, women were encouraged to enter examples of their domestic efforts in competitions, and by the middle of the century quilt competitions came to take pride of place in fairs.

The Era of the Association

While conditions on the frontier provided a unique domestic setting for pioneer families, industrial development in the East and Midwest ensured the funds to support a fast-paced social mobility for many families. Mid-nineteenth-century evangelists were quick to bemoan money getting, which was seen as disruptive to family ties. Methodists, Congregationalists, Presbyterians, Unitarians, and Baptists organized a diverse array of ecumenical societies in order both to bring about moral reform, teach Republican virtue, and Christian piety in the new society.

This period has been referred to as the era of the association, for along with the church and the family, the association became the third pillar of middle-class life. Many of these associations, spurred on by the spirit of reform, were created to promote good causes such as establishing schools and institutions for the deaf and blind, helping orphans, or to combat social evils like drinking and slavery. Many had female auxiliaries which ultimately were more active than the men's branches, especially the Temperance (first formed in 1808) and the Anti-Slavery societies.

Women were called upon to play the dual role of keeper of the hearth and virtuous reformer. This led to the creation of a number of benevolent societies associated with women and the church. There were Sewing Circles, Sewing Societies, Female Prayer Groups, Women's Guilds, Fancy Work Improvement Clubs, Ladies' Aid Societies, and African Dorcas societies in black churches.

These groups took it upon themselves to do needlework and, in particular, to make quilts for worthy causes. Many of these quilts were made to send to western missionaries or to auction for some charitable purpose. Symbolism in needlework reached new heights, and female anti-slavery societies held fairs and bazaars where they sold needlework products to raise money for the growing abolitionist movement. In this pre-Civil War period, quiltmakers developed specific patterns that dealt with the question of slavery and abolition, such as Slave Chain (earlier called Job's Tears), and Underground Railroad. The fundraising quilt became an important concept which assumed a national urgency during the Civil War when quilts were auctioned to raise money for the troops, and thousands of quilts were made by women across the country and distributed to soldiers in desperate need of proper bedding.

Impact of New Technology

Synthetic Dyes

The discovery of synthetic dyes by the English chemist William Henry Perkin in 1856, and their subsequent production in Germany, stimulated the output of the commercial textile industry which now began widespread roller printing of brightly colored cotton fabric. Although various kinds of wools, including twills and challis, continued to be used along with cotton-and-linen combinations, cotton became the predominant material for quilts. There were widely varied patterns on the cotton fabrics, which included rainbow prints, prints with small-scale sprigs and berries, polka dots printed in vibrant reds, blues, greens and browns, and new and more decorative color combinations of pistachio, lavender, and various shades of lime. This new palette of color and design allowed women to create quilts featuring contrasts of increased subtlety in their overall patterns.

The Sewing Machine

One of the most important inventions which contributed to the growth and continuation of the quilting tradition was the sewing machine. Developed during the 1840s and 1850s by Isaac Merrit Singer, it saved women hours of time-consuming hand piecework.

The high price of the sewing machine precluded its widespread distribution and most sales went to clothing manufacturers. However, at the end of the Civil War in 1865, the sewing machine companies, anxious to establish a domestic market, recognized that they needed to counter two widespread beliefs which stood in the way of sales: "the first that women couldn't control machinery, and second, that, freed from some of their arduous labors, women would go wild…people believed that men had the intelligence and temperament for machines;

women, those delicate creatures, could use tools (needles, brooms, washboards) but not machines."[4]

The battle to domesticate the sewing machine was taken on by its manufacturing companies and one of the first national advertising campaigns was the result. The machine was seen in thousands of pictures and trade cards as a labor-saving device which would free women from hours of unnecessary toil.

Following the success of this campaign, the sewing machine slowly became affordable to the average family, due in part to the development of new credit facilities. The ownership of a sewing machine became a symbol of prestige. Bedding as well as clothing came to be stitched on the machine and more and more women experimented with machine sewing on quilts.

Left: Professional photographers regularly traveled across the plains and prairies taking pictures of settlers, and these pictures were frequently sent back East to other relatives and friends. The sewing machine, often the most expensive possession of the household, was regularly hauled outside where family members proudly posed around the "Singer."

The Civil War

With the onset of the Civil War in 1862, thousands of women turned their hands away from making domestic furnishings and fashion to devote their time and talents to the war cause. Both Union (northern) and Confederate (southern) women participated in relief efforts, supplying food, clothing, and bedding to the armies. Hope chests and linen closets were raided as women went around door-to-door collecting sheets, quilts, and blankets. Quilts that had been family heirlooms, as well as roughly quilted or tied everyday bedcoverings, were turned over to army supply units. The impact of the war saw quiltmaking taken up by thousands of women as a patriotic responsibility, and in the North new quilting patterns for the Union army were published in several women's magazines.

Great fundraising Sanitary Commission fairs were organized by women in cities like Chicago, St Louis, Brooklyn, Long Island, and New York City. These fairs became well-attended social events, held in elaborately decorated halls containing booths and exhibition spaces. Homemade products which included all varieties of food and fancy needlework (most prominently the quilt) raised a remarkable total of $4,500,000 for northern war relief. Virginia Gunn describes how at the Brooklyn Fair there was a replica of a New England farmhouse complete with tableau events which included an old-fashioned quilting party, and New York City's Metropolitan Fair presented a quilting party tableau.

The fairs, along with other fundraising events organized by women, created a widespread national impact. Newspapers, which had ignored women's activism at the beginning of the war, began to carry regular announcements and reports of the meetings of Ladies' Aid Societies. When Burlington, Iowa, staged a successful benefit concert in 1863, the local newspaper reported it in full, commenting that "the ladies…not only deserve the gratitude of the soldiers but the thanks of the community."

Fashion and the Quilt

After the Civil War, fashionable American women saw quiltmaking as an activity linked to the romance of rural life and bygone days. The rise of a ready-to-wear clothing market and factory-produced goods created an association between the handmade quilt and the past.

The new democratization of dress had a double-edged effect. On one hand it stimulated the continuation of a tradition of dress and custom among women in thousands of small towns and farms on the prairies and plains of the frontier—these women could now order a readymade calico gown or bonnet from new mail order catalogues.

It also played a role in creating a society increasingly concerned with fashion, style, and money; middle- and upper-class women living in prosperous urban centers and southern plantations insisted that their wardrobes be created out of imported silks. The silk dress became the fashionable and desired attire in which to entertain in one's elaborate Victorian-style parlor. By the end of the nineteenth century the quilt, made of both calico and silk, was also expressing these two trends.

Left: Detail of Victorian Crazy Crib Quilt, c. 1890, American, 18 x 24 in. (46 x 61 cm). This crazy quilt is unusual in that it has both nine-patch blocks and a medallion center, which set it apart from other crazy quilts of the day. It is highly embroidered, and is made of luxurious fabrics. For more information about this quilt, see page 110.

4 The Age of Expansion

American concepts of taste and design during the final years of the nineteenth century reflected larger social and economic events. A wide geographic media network of newspapers, periodicals, broadsides, and magazines—many targeted at a female readership—guaranteed the spread of new ideas. The development of mail order houses like Sears and Roebuck and Montgomery Ward insured that women, even in remote rural environments, could receive through the mail the latest fashion, fabric or appliance, including the majority of materials necessary for making a quilt—from a thimble to a sewing machine.

New Directions in Quiltmaking

By the last half of the nineteenth century quiltmaking had evolved in two main directions, both fueled by a growing emphasis on artistic taste, fashion, and patriotism. On one hand, there was a widespread development of ingenious new designs as calico piecework became increasingly complex. Intricate patterns like Ocean Waves and Drunkard's Path, and sentimental and figurative patterns such as Little Red Schoolhouse, Tree of Life, Horseshoe, and Butterfly quilts were made out of a wide variety of cotton prints. "The cut of the late-nineteenth-century fashion styles—with their large sleeves, flowing skirts, and bustles—created leftover fabric scraps, and since women continually updated their wardrobes, they accumulated a large variety of these pieces. Thrifty and practical women utilized them in pieced quilt block designs, even though they could purchase inexpensive fabric."[5] The Ocean Waves quilt pictured on page 192 reveals the kind of detailed piecework which was becoming popular at this time.

On the other hand, silk had become paramount in the fashion world and women found it imperative to have at least one good silk dress. The opening of treaty ports with China and the domestic production of silk made this a realistic desire, and soon the high status of silk was applied to furnishings, and women all over America aspired to display fancy silk needlework in their homes.

The Decorative Arts Movement, transplanted from Britain, had re-established earlier English traditions of detailed and inventive embroidery as a praiseworthy feminine pastime, and stimulated the development of a new genre of quilt altogether. The crazy quilt was a random assortment of irregular silk, velvet or rich brocade patches (fabrics now readily and cheaply available) which were rather eloquently stitched together with brightly colored silk embroidery thread, often with over 100 different kinds of stitches in one piece.

Technological developments also continued to play an important role in enriching American quiltmaking. Advances in colorfast sharp dyes and roller printing created a vivid assortment of new fabrics and colors, and even though increased factory output sometimes meant a decrease in fabric quality, women continued to be stimulated by the Calico Craze. Charm quilts which were composed of 999 pieces cut out of the same template but in which there were no identical fabrics, became very popular, as did the Postage Stamp quilt made of thousands of squares which were less than 1 inch (2.5 cm) apiece.

The Growing Middle Classes

By the late nineteenth century, child-care and homemaking had become a full-time job for the urban middle-class woman. She was no longer expected to make a direct contribution to family income, but was to be supported by her male relatives. Being able to support a woman in comparative leisure and not needing to depend on her wages became a significant criterion of a man's membership of the middle class. The ready availability of domestic service, often supplied by immigrants such as the Irish in New York, meant that middle-class women had far more time to devote to other domestic activities. The preoccupation with the beautiful and artistic home was continually encouraged by the popular media.

The national concern about design was informed in part by new scientific discoveries, and in particular by the investigation of optical illusion which accompanied advances in photography. This preoccupation is reflected in quilts of the period in which a two-dimensional surface appears three-dimensional. Patterns such as Stairway to Heaven and Windmill Blades were fashioned out of silk and velvet, cottons, and wools.

National taste was also strongly influenced by exposure to Eastern cultures, resulting in a host of decorative objects such as wallpaper and textiles resplendent with Oriental motifs. Quilts such as the Fan quilt and the Quill quilt, made up of brightly colored scraps, approximately two inches wide and one inch deep, sewn into overlapping rows of quills, are examples of a strong Japanese influence.

Patriotic Fervor

The American Centennial in 1876, the huge exposition in Philadelphia which celebrated 100 years of nationhood, ignited a commercial and domestic fashion for American symbols. Special cotton prints were manufactured which displayed commemorative patterns such as liberty bells, liberty caps, profiles of George Washington and bombs bursting in the air. Patriotic quilts proudly bearing Federal Eagles, stars, stripes, pictures of presidents, and names of states were enormously popular.

Quilts, as in earlier years, symbolized domestic and public events. Marriages, births, and deaths were commemorated in innumerable Brides' quilts, Crib quilts, and Mourning quilts. Quilt patterns were named after war heroes, such as Dewey's Dream for Admiral Dewey in commemoration of the Spanish-American War. Others, like the T-Block, were associated with causes like the temperance movement. Outline quilts, also inspired by the decorative arts craze, depicted in bright thread against a white background a pictorial or historical motif.

Right: Detail of *Patriotic Crazy Quilt*, American, twentieth century. Here the American flag is surrounded by colorful embroidered detail and a network of interlocking shapes. The full quilt appears on page 114.

Backed by tremendous financial gains and a growing overseas trade network, America began to have a strong voice in foreign affairs. For the first time, Americans saw themselves as part of an international community. The 1876 Centennial celebrations not only featured impressive displays extolling American advances in areas such as electricity, internal combustion, and steam power, but also hosted tremendously popular exhibitions by fifty-six foreign nations. The Japanese Pavilion, an elaborate and sumptuous display of textiles, bronzes, embroideries, and silks, and the exhibition of the Royal School of Art Needlework from Kensington, England, were two of the best received events. Both were to have an enormous influence in setting new standards of taste for the American home.

These influences were quickly translated into a domestic setting through magazines like the newly formed *Ladies Home Journal*, *Home Beautiful*, and new journals devoted to household and decorative arts. Women were advised that good taste and artistic discernment need not be limited to the wealthy, and that women of all stations could, by their own labor and handiwork, create a beautiful and artistically furnished home.

Although these magazines were intended for the intelligent middle-class housewife, the ideas which they espoused found their way to a much wider readership of lower-class and rural women. The calico quilt, which had featured so strongly in the lives of countless American women, was deemed unworthy in the 1870s and 1880s for consideration in the well-appointed home. An article in *Household Magazine* in 1875, entitled "Beds and Bedrooms," makes the admonishment clear: "Neither the unhealthy thing called a comfortable nor the unsightly covering known as the patched quilt should be seen on a bed in this day." A host of articles and features designed to illuminate women's understanding about the tasteful Victorian style and to raise standards of housekeeping rejected traditional calico patchwork in favor of decorative embroidery. The silk quilt or show quilt which followed is considered to be a grass-roots response to the fervor surrounding the Decorative Arts Movement. These sumptuous quilts, more decorative than to be used for warmth, often sported intricately embroidered motifs such as names, butterflies, and flowers, and included beading, ribbons, sequins, and chenille appliqués.

Quilts and the Decorative Arts Movement

The Decorative Arts Movement, an English phenomenon inspired by the writings and work of William Morris, John Ruskin and their followers, was embraced by American society with great enthusiasm. Formally introduced during the Centennial Exposition in 1876 through an exhibition of decorative needlework presented by the Royal School of Art Needlework, this aesthetic movement popularized the concepts which united domesticity, morality, and art, emphasizing that decorative objects for the home must demonstrate "clearness of form coupled with the mystery that comes from abundance and richness of detail."[6]

The women who founded the Kensington Royal School of Art Needlework in 1872 intended both to recreate the tradition of ornamental needlework and to provide needy gentlewomen with suitable employment. This idea had a strong appeal in America where the economic crisis during and immediately after the Civil War had created short-term financial difficulties for many middle-class women.

The American Crazy Quilt

American quiltmaking traditions, which had grown and developed over the previous 150 years, refused to adhere to fashion dictates.

Nonetheless the decorative arts fad was so strong, that by the late 1870s the quilt had begun to adapt to popular aesthetics.

A few years later, a number of magazines noted this growing trend. *Harper's Bazaar* wrote: "We have discarded in our modern quilts the regular geometric design once so popular, and substituted what are more like the changing figures of the kaleidoscope, or the beauty and infinite variety of oriental mosaics."

The crazy quilt, which combined the Oriental notion of asymmetry with decorative arts embroidery techniques and concepts of individuality, quickly became the darling of the fashion world. These new-style silk quilts, made for decoration, were as well suited to the parlor as to the bedroom. This trend was encouraged and indeed strongly supported by a host of important women's magazines.

Harper's wrote that the crazy quilt "deserves to be handed down as an heirloom." *Dorcas* magazine explained: "Of all the 'crazes' which have swept over and fairly engulfed us, there is none which has taken a deeper hold upon the fair women of our land than this one of the crazy patchwork...Many a woman with strong artistic taste finds no other outlet for it than in work such as this."

Quilt Patterns

There were literally thousands of named quilt designs which, by
the end of the century, were known to a wide range of women in
states and territories across the country. Many of these patterns had
developed from basic designs through individual variation or by
unaccounted-for changes as a pattern passed from region to region
and from state to state. Before the widespread publication of quilt
patterns in the early twentieth century, many designs were reproduced
from memory by an increasingly transient society, which perhaps
accounts for some of the variations. What was known as Flying
Dutchman in one area became Indian Trail in another. The Bear's
Paw in Ohio or Kentucky became Duck's Foot in the Mud in Long
Island, and Hand of Friendship in Philadelphia.

While many quilt names were rooted in factual events like
Whigs' Defeat or Burgoyne's Surrender, others such as Glorified
Nine-Patch, Dove in the Window, or Fish in a Dish conveyed a sense
of romantic whimsy. The personal name which might have been given
to a pattern developed by an otherwise anonymous maker became
almost legendary when passed down though her family, or circulated
among her neighbors. This can be observed in patterns such as Aunt

Sukey's Choice, Aunt Vinah's Favorite, or Flo's Fan. Many patterns, such as Candlelight or Tangled Briar, have been lost to history, while others have been carefully researched by catalogue companies. Some were renamed specifically for twentieth-century consumption, like the old English-style Hexagon or Mosaic which became Grandma's Flower Garden. According to quilt historians Patsy and Myron Orlofsky, certain names changed over the years depending upon the issues of concern to quilters at any one time. Job's Tears, originally a religious name in the first quarter of the nineteenth century, changed to Slave Chain by 1825 when the issue of slavery was on people's minds. When Texas was annexed in 1840 the same pattern became Texas Tears, and after 1865 it was known as Rocky Road to Kansas or Kansas Troubles. Finally, during the third quarter of the century it was called Endless Chain.

One of the most well-loved and handsome patterns was based on the lily. Often composed with diamond blocks, it was an extremely popular pattern that migrated across the continent bearing a variety of names to suit new locales. In northern New England it was Meadow Lily, in Pennsylvania it was Tiger Lily. It was called North Carolina Lily all through the South, except in Kentucky and Tennessee where it was known as Mountain Lily. It was named for the Fire Lily in Ohio, Indiana and Illinois, the Prairie Lily west of the Mississippi, and the Mariposa Lily beyond the Rocky Mountains.

Individual Significance

Quilt names endowed a handcrafted piece of needlework with personal meaning and were inspired by a wide range of experiences. Religion, domestic life, the community, nature, work, politics, and literature were reflected in thousands of expressive and often lyrical pattern names. Religious names included Cross and Crown, Jacob's Ladder, Coronation, Wonder of the World, and David and Goliath. Common or domestic objects such as the Monkey Wrench, Churndash, Cake Stand, Cherry Basket, and Carpenter's Wheel were all part of the quilt vocabulary. Games and puzzles such as Yankee Puzzle, Merry-Go-Round, and Leapfrog, community events like Barn Raising, and particular square dance calls like Virginia Reel, Swing-in-the-Corner, or Hands All Around were memorialized in graphically descriptive names. Significant buildings such as churches, schoolhouses, and log cabins were stitched into a host of figurative patterns. The Schoolhouse Quilt was a popular motif well into the twentieth century.

Traditional design motifs based on natural elements continued to inspire America's quilters. Flowers such as the rose formed a complete genre of pattern names including Whig Rose, Harrison Rose, Democratic Rose, Rose Wreath, Rosebud, Rosedream, Rose of Sharon, and Ohio Rose among others. Love Apple, Kentucky Flower Pot, Hickory Leaf, Morning Glory, Indian Plum, Grapes and Vines, Iris, Tea Leaf, Dogwood, Corn and Beans, and Field of Daisies, are only a few of the multitude of botanical names which were translated into quilt patterns. Birds, animals, and insects were well represented too, with myriad designs such as Spider's Web, Snake's Trail, Flying Geese, Swarm of Bees, Turkey Tracks, Bunnies, and Swallows' Flight. The Bluebird Appliqué, Snail Trail, and Bear's Paw Quilts are well-loved designs created by thousands of women over the years.

The movement of the sun, moon, and stars was captured in titles like Moon and Stars, Rolling Star Starburst, Falling Star, Half Moon Rising, Twinkling Star, Big Dipper, and Rising Sun.

Symbolism

Many designs, whether geometric, figurative or abstract, conveyed a host of associated and symbolic meanings which were understood through custom. Pineapples stitched into a quilt (or carved on a gatepost) stood for hospitality, while a pomegranate meant abundance. Rings and hearts were clearly to do with love and courtship. Trees have long been associated with Christianity, and the Pine Tree pattern in particular was alternately referred to as the Tree of Plenty and the Tree Everlasting. In times of pioneer settlement in the sometimes inhospitable West, it came to represent the pine forests of New England; many settlers, after building their sod hut or log cabin, would plant a pine tree to be reminded of home.

The Log Cabin quilt was made from the middle of the nineteenth century in any one of six different designs: Barn Raising, Straight Furrow, Courthouse Steps, Streak of Lightning, Light and Dark, and Pineapple or Windmill. The names in this instance relate to a visual metaphor, with the choice of scale, color, and fabric completely altering the final effect. The Pineapple Log Cabin and the Light and Dark variation are as different as night and day. The Log Cabin quilt was strongly associated with Abraham Lincoln's Log Cabin campaign, in which he stood for rural, honest, pioneer ideas, while the traditional red center symbolized the domestic hearth.

Names relating to social rituals like love and marriage come down to us in a legacy of patterns such as Young Man's Fancy, Double Wedding Ring, Bridal Stairway, Lover's Knot, Old Man's Ramble, Wedding Knot, and Widower's Choice. Other names related to politics, such as Washington's Plumes, Union Quilt, Clay's Choice, and President's Wreath; or literature, for example Delectable Mountains (from John Bunyan's *Pilgrim's Progress*), and Lady of the Lake (from Sir Walter Scott's poem). It seems that although a woman might have remained at home, her sensibilities and concerns embraced a wider world.

Ethnic Communities

There were also a number of characteristic quilts produced by particular regional or ethnic groups, in addition to the Amish and European sects. While these quilts often share features with mainstream quilts, they do reflect the special concerns, beliefs or aspirations of the communities which made them.

Hawaiian quilts are characterized by their central medallion format and highly contrasted appliquéd patterns made from folded cut-paper designs, often based on native plants, flags, and symbols of royalty.

60

A combination of native art motifs and missionary-inspired traditional cotton quilting techniques gave rise to these uniquely crafted quilts.

The German settlers who emigrated to Pennsylvania learned the tradition of quilting from their neighbors from the British Isles. They tended to create quilts mostly out of red and green on a white background; when a third color was added it was either yellow or orange or possibly pink. Popular motifs included tulips, birds, and hearts, and appliqué flower patterns such as Rose Wreath, Cockscomb and Currant, and Peony among others. Often these would be arranged in quarters or smaller blocks. There are few Pennsylvanian German quilts which can be documented before 1850, since until this period families in the communities preferred the German-style feather beds and comforters to quilts.

Afro-American quilts reflect both an American and an African heritage. Popular perceptions of these quilts, however, often end up as stereotypes which are not accurate. Black people have been in America

Right: This picture shows a family making a *Dresden Plate* quilt. The room is papered with newspaper cuttings, patterns, and pictures cut from magazines.

for many generations; they fought in the Revolutionary and Civil Wars, helped to settle the frontier, and formed stable communities throughout the country, and many black quilt designs reflect this American heritage. Nevertheless, a segment of documented black quilts also reflects African influences, including the use of vivid color combinations, irregular piecing, big stitches, and multiple patterns.

Probably the best-known of those quilts created by black American women which have been documented is one made by the former slave Harriet Powers, in Georgia in 1895. Called *Creation of the Animals*, it contains a series of fifteen appliquéd blocks depicting a narrative based on biblical motifs. This remarkable quilt, now in the Museum of Fine Arts in Boston, is said to be reminiscent of traditional appliquéd textiles from Dahomey in West Africa.

Amish Quilts

The Amish and Mennonite sects created one of the best known, and most distinctive bodies of American quilts. Amish quilts are noted for quality of craftsmanship, and their heightened use of color and design, expressive of a history and culture particular to the Amish people.

The Amish, or Plain People, are an Anabaptist sect that broke from the Swiss Mennonite movement in the 1690s. Determined to hold themselves aloof from the vanities of the outside world and to model themselves on the early pure Christians, they emigrated from southern Germany to America during the nineteenth century at the invitation of William Penn. Like many other religious groups they settled in Pennsylvania, but unlike any other Pennsylvania Dutch immigrants, the Amish managed to maintain a strong sense of faith and community spirit over successive generations.

The rules of the Amish social order are provided by the *Ordnung* (pronounced ott-ning), are still followed to a greater or lesser degree by all members. Basic rules concerning dress and the use of decoration in the home are set out in the first part of the *Ordnung*. For example: "There shall be no display in houses, namely when the houses are built or painted, with various colors or filled with showy furniture…not to make such proud kinds of furniture and not to decorate them with such loud or gay colors…No ornamental, bright, showy, form fitting, immodest or silk like clothing…dress coats…to be black only… dress socks to be black…hats to be black…no pressed trousers… women to wear shawls, bonnets or caps in public."

The second part of the *Ordnung* is the set of understood customs and traditions governing all aspects of daily life; these vary among sects and regions.

By the second half of the nineteenth century, the Amish had begun to form communities throughout the Midwest, and by the 1860s they began to acquire the American penchant for quiltmaking, as part of a general exchange of ideas, goods, and practices between themselves group of women at a frolic or bee.

Shunning what they felt to be frivolous, the Amish generally avoided appliqué on their quilts, and printed fabrics, if used, were restricted to the backing material. Yet they used elaborate quilting patterns that kept the filling in place, an addition both decorative and functional. These quilting designs—from the loose feather to the basket and the multi-pointed star—deliberately play off against the patterns of the colors. There is some evidence that the ornamental stitching patterns used by the Amish were influenced by the gay appliquéd motifs of the quilts created by their Pennsylvanian German, non-Amish neighbors, but without their reds and yellows.

Right: *Diamond in a Square*, Amish, American, 1920s. This quilt sports a characteristically simple pachwork design, with beautifully quilted patterns on the panels.

5 The Twentieth Century

The cotton quilt, which had suffered from the vagaries of fashion in the 1870s and 1880s, was now widely embraced as part of the sentiment connected to the Colonial Revival Movement. This national revival celebrated pioneer life and presented a romantic image of the Colonial past with stable social relationships and ethnic and cultural homogeneity.

By the turn of the century, the country was ablaze with patriotic fervor and the simple life of the early settlers—from the Pilgrims through to Thomas Jefferson—was represented as wholesome, pure, and commendable. A *Harper's Bazaar* article in 1905 noted that the American woman had "made herself acquainted with the lives of her Colonial and Revolutionary ancestors."

At the same time, however, in stark contrast to the fife and drums of the Revolutionary past, a modern consumer ethic was developing, for, by the early twentieth century, American industry had flooded the market with a host of consumer delights. From clothing to appliances, toothpaste, and socks, Americans were buying and using a heretofore unheard-of number of goods. By 1928 almost two out of every three families owned an automobile and one out of three had a radio. National and state expenditures on education, the arts, medical and scientific research, and social charities reached record levels. The advertising industry successfully sold the plentiful products of this new large-scale mass production to the public.

The idealization of the past, of home and hearth, simple times and rural pleasures, characterized liberal thinking in early twentieth-century America. New styles of art and architecture, many rooted in the decorative art tradition, strongly influenced quilt designs. Both the Art Nouveau style of the 1900s and the Art Deco style of the 1920s and 1930s adapted easily to pieced and appliquéd quilt patterns.

Thus, the influence of these social and economic trends stimulated twentieth-century quiltmaking practices. The quilt had now become both a symbol of a rich Colonial heritage and a testament to a woman's ability to create an artistic personal statement. As the national fashion for quiltmaking grew, the quilt came to be part of a larger commercial network.

The Quilt Industry and the Media

At the turn of the century, quilt designs became popularized on a commercial basis for the first time. In 1898 new catalogue companies, such as the St Louis, Missouri-based Ladies' Art Company, had begun publication of inexpensive books of quilt patterns and instructions. Researchers in these companies worked to rediscover, document, and publish traditional patterns.

Women artists and designers, many professionally trained, developed a multitude of new patterns which both adapted older designs to the popular Art-Deco fashion and created entirely original patterns in a range of sparkling new textiles. The older dark fabrics of the turn of the century, which bore sober little geometrics and sprig-like prints, were replaced by the mid-1920s with jazzy-looking, large floral motifs, Art-Deco designs, and pastels in new sherbet shades of lilac, raspberry, turquoise, and green.

Companies which manufactured products associated with quiltmaking—cotton, thread, batting (wadding), etc.—advertised heavily in publications targeted for a female readership. These magazines, journals and, later, newspapers promoted a multitude of new patterns in numerous articles and features.

Crib and children's quilts were produced which featured for the first time motifs such as fairy tale and nursery rhyme characters, toys, animals, and alphabets. One of the best known, specifically twentieth-century designs is the childlike Sunbonnet Sue.

Several designs of this period were created to suit the sentimental temperament of the twentieth-century woman. These included the popular Double Wedding Ring, the Dresden Plate, and Grandma's Fan. The Grandmother's Flower Garden quilt pictured on page 98 is an ingenious three-dimensional reinterpretation of the traditional English Hexagon coupled with the Tumbling Blocks pattern.

The *Ladies Home Journal* was one of the most important of the women's magazines, and by 1910 it had reached a circulation of nearly 2 million readers. Edward Bok, its influential editor, advocated a return to the traditions of simplicity and domesticity for women. For him a woman's place was still in the home. "My idea," he wrote, "is to keep women at home, especially as there are enough writers who are trying to take her out of it."

Bok instituted a department called "How Much Can be Done with Little" in an effort to provide practical tips for simple living. Features such as "How We Can Live a Simple Life, by an American Mother,"

"How to Live Cheaply," and "A Lesson in Plain Sewing" were all intended to distance women from decades of ornate Victoriana. "The curse of the American woman today is useless bric-a-brac," wrote Bok in 1900. Like other editors, he strongly supported the Arts and Crafts Movement and observed in 1901 that a "William Morris craze has been developing, and it is a fad we cannot push with too much vigor."

Marie Webster, the prominent needlework editor of the *Ladies Home Journal* in 1915 wrote the first substantial book about quilts, entitled *Quilts, Their Story and How to Make Them*. She not only pointed to the value of the handmade over the machine-manufactured, but went on to equate quiltmaking with patriotism.

The Progressive Era

The scandals, public corruption, and general immorality of the gilded last years of the previous century were publicly condemned at the highest levels. President Theodore Roosevelt, writing in his autobiography in 1913, noted that the industrial and financial revolutions had provoked a "riot of individual materialism, under which complete freedom for the individual…turned out in practice to mean perfect freedom for the strong to wrong the weak."

The cultural nationalism that was expressed by the Colonial Revival Movement carried on in force for most of the first half of the twentieth century and the fashion for Colonial decoration and, in particular, for the handmade quilt continued unabated. There were many reasons why this movement was so deeply rooted, why it didn't fade away or shift out of fashion like previous styles. One reason was that America needed an embracing set of ideas to temper the excesses of industrial expansion and radicalism. Another was to assure middle-class, white America that the tremendous influx of immigrants wouldn't interfere with the dominant American culture. The First World War created the backdrop for a renewed national identity and need for patriotism, while the onset of the Depression years gave rise to the widespread and reassuring imagery connected to traditional home values and rural America.

Published Quilt Patterns and Exhibitions

Despite all the popular pressures and influences upon quilters, older established traditions remained unchanged. Women continued, as their mothers and grandmothers before them, to go to church guilds and other organizations and quilt together. Many other women, heedless of fashion, carried on individually making quilts in a variety of calico prints and designs.

The old custom of local women getting together to quilt was in fact reinforced by all of the quilting information in the media. Farm journals such as *The Progressive Farmer*, *The National Stockman*, and *Farm and Fireside*, as well as home decorating and fashion publications like *Good Housekeeping*, *Hearth and Home*, and *Better Homes and Gardens*, had all, by the 1920s, begun the widespread publication of printed patterns and instructions. Many of these were taken up by local groups.

The idea of printing patterns was not a new one. English magazines of the nineteenth century such as *The Family Friend*, and books such as *Treasures in Needlework*, had published a number of patterns and instructions which were copied by the American magazine *Godey's* and later by both *Graham's* and *Peterson's* magazines. In the crazy quilt years, magazines and journals such as *Art Amateur* published detailed descriptions of how to make a crazy quilt. What was new, however, was the commercialization of the quilt pattern industry.

These early published patterns were produced by providing quilters with large sheets of paper with the actual design printed on them.

This was then traced and transferred onto a piece of heavy paper which was used as a template. Advances in techniques soon led, in the early 1900s, to methods where a pattern could be transferred onto fabric simply by running a hot iron over it. The commercialization of quilting led companies to an ongoing search for new products and new designs. An advertisement from a 1933 edition of the *Knoxville News Sentinel* exclaims about a new cold-transfer method called "The Wonder Package," which offered readers: "No more hot irons—no more waste!" Sears, Roebuck and Company offered perforated quilting patterns and stamping wax: "No more tiresome marking of quilts in the old-fashioned way."

Pattern Designers

A new development in twentieth-century quilting which followed from the publication of commercial patterns was the promotion of a number of women artists who created individual and distinct designs. The names are associated with their companies: Marie Webster, Anne Orr, Rose Kretsinger, and Ruby Short McKim, among others. The designs were not only published by the artists themselves, but were also used by various syndication companies and the batting manufacturers.

Marie Webster's designs were very much influenced by Art Nouveau ideas. She tended to create floral motifs in a more linear flowing style coupled with new pastel shades. Her well-known patterns included Sunflowers, Dogwood, Grapes and Vines, Indiana Wreath, Irises, Poppies, and the intricate Tree of Life.

The quilts favored by Anne Orr were mainly floral appliqués of soft pastel fabrics stitched onto light backgrounds. Often these would be in the central medallion style reminiscent of the Colonial period and finished with a scalloped edge. Designs included the Jonquil, Nosegay, and Poppy. Anne Orr was also well known for a series of intricate, pieced floral and basket patterns which resembled cross-stitched embroidery. The French Wreath and Heirloom Basket were two of her most popular patterns.

Ruby Short McKim, Art-Needlework editor for *Better Homes and Gardens*, published a number of inspired designs from her studio in Independence, Missouri.

By the 1920s, newspapers began to feature quilt columns in their Saturday and Sunday editions. These features were either locally produced or part of a national syndication network, and by 1934 more than 400 newspapers included such columns. *The Chicago*

Tribune, *The Kansas City Star*, and *The Rural New Yorker* were among those papers which published hundreds of patterns over the years. Many of these appeared under apple pie names like Aunt Martha or Grandmother Clark. The most well known of the designers who produced patterns for newspapers was Laura Wheeler, whose designs were syndicated through the Old Chelsea Station Needlecraft Service of New York. Her patterns were popular because often they were pieced, which encouraged women to use up old scraps.

Quilt kits were introduced during the 1920s and 1930s, by a number of firms, including the Ladies' Art Company, in 1922. The more expensive kits would include a cotton sheet with the appropriate design stamped on it as well as the quilting lines, and pieces of pre-cut, color-sorted fabric were also included. For example, a Pansy appliqué kit available from *Needlecraft Magazine* included a piece of cotton sheet stamped with appliqué placements and quilting lines.

The Western motif which inspired the Cowboy quilt on page 200 may very well have been the result of a purchased kit pattern. The detailed appliqué work and the subtle coloring artfully contrived to produce the effect of shadows strongly suggest either the hand of an expert needlewoman, or a kit. Published patterns, quilt kits and successful quilt designers all represented a new era in quiltmaking where patterns became associated with artists rather than evolving through processes of historical anonymity.

However, there were many other patterns popular during the last century which are unattributable. Many of these designs were interpretations of everyday items, such as had been the practice in the nineteenth century. However, instead of churndashes and cakestands, there were umbrellas and coffee cups; popular and somewhat obscure animal motifs included turtles, birds, and Scottie dogs, as well as purely graphic designs. One of the most interesting genre of twentieth-century quilts was that related to national events and people.

Right: *Sunflowers*, 74 x 84 in. (188 x 213 cm) American, c.1921. This highly stylized pattern was designed by Mrs Marie Webster, needlework editor of *Ladies Home Journal*.

Exhibitions and Contests

By the twentieth century quilts, as well as other forms of American folk art, were also beginning to be shown at exhibitions and taken more seriously as cultural artefacts. The Newark Museum featured quilts in a show in 1914, followed by one at the University of Kansas in 1920. Quilts also continued to be presented in contests in both agricultural and county fairs. Stearns and Foster, along with department stores and other commercial enterprises directly connected to sewing, sponsored enormously popular quilt contests during the 1930s. The commercialization of quiltmaking encouraged a huge audience of quilt enthusiasts and, for the first time, a major contest was held at national level. This most spectacular quilt display was one of the main features of the Chicago Exposition in 1933 which was entitled the Century of Progress. A rather brilliant marketing strategy was conceived by Sears, Roebuck and Company who initiated a nationwide quilt contest six months before the fair, offering prize money of $7,500. Over 25,000 women entered their quilts at regional Sears branches.

These quilts were then judged by regional panels of local quilt and art authorities, and thirty of the winning quilts were put on display at the magnificent Sears Building exhibit just inside the fair grounds.

The prize for the winning quilt, an Eight-Point Combination Feathered Star made by Margaret Rogers Caden, was handed out by no less a luminary than First Lady Eleanor Roosevelt. Naturally this generated unprecedented publicity and business for Sears, and inspired other manufacturers to sponsor similar events on a mostly local level through department stores. Quilts had become part of America's big-time business. But as the war years drew closer, women's interests turned to other more pressing considerations.

By the 1940s, the fad for quilting began to diminish. With America becoming involved in the Second World War, women were called upon in large numbers to join the workforce. As both time and fabric became scarce there seemed to be less and less reason to make quilts. Although quilting certainly continued locally among women all over America, it wasn't until thirty years later, in the early 1970s, that quilts were once more to gain national attention when new, aesthetic considerations previously applied to paintings were now directed to quilts.

Conclusion

By the twentieth century, quiltmaking had come to acquire a grassroots force of its own. It had evolved its own folklore, its own symbols, and its own traditions which were passed down verbally, or by example, through families, and exchanged among communities. American life as experienced by women—personal and social, material and spiritual, everyday and artistic—had been stitched into a remarkable legacy. And whether pieced, embroidered or appliquéd, quilts came to reflect the enduring spirit of women. With their profusion of colors, fabrics, and detailed stitchery, quilts can be read as a kind of textile journal.

Quiltmaking in America has been subject to many influences over the years. Economics, politics, religion, and technology as well as cultural ideas have all played a role in defining the history of the American quilt. But while these trends were certainly a part of a woman's daily experience, the greater or lesser individual act of creativity, out of which every quilt was fashioned, came from the same timeless impulse that informs any work of art.

From the delicate chintz and flowered quilts of the eighteenth century, the heavy woolen Log Cabins of the 1860s, and silk Crazies of the 1880s, to the airplanes and sailors of the twentieth century, quilts imbue American history with both a social and visual dimension. Nowhere else do quilted bedcoverings show the degree of skill and originality seen in American quilts. For indeed quilts are more than decorative covers, they are genuine documents that illustrate the irrepressible creativity of generations of American women.

Bibliography

1 Brackman, Barbara. *Clues in the Calico*. EPM Publications, Inc., McLean, Virginia, 1989.

2 and 3 Keber, Linda K. and Jane De Hart Mathews. *Women's America: Refocusing the Past*. Oxford University Press, New York. 1982.

4 Garoutte, Sally and Laurel Horton (Eds.) *Uncoverings*. American Quilt Study Group, Mill Valley, California. Vols 1–10, 1980–89.

5 Lasansky, Jeannette. *Bits and Pieces: Textile Traditions*. Oral Traditions Project, Lewisburg, Pennsylvania. 1991.

6 Thompson E. P. William Morris: *Romantic to Revolutionary*. Merlin Press, London. 1955

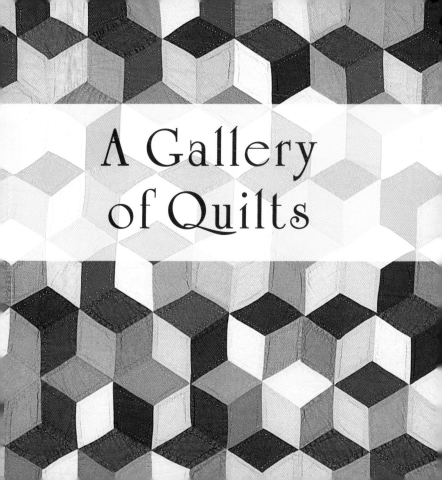

A Gallery of Quilts

Young Man's Fancy

c. 1900

New England, USA

55 x 70 in. (140 x 178 cm)

PRIVATE COLLECTION

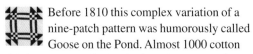 Before 1810 this complex variation of a nine-patch pattern was humorously called Goose on the Pond. Almost 1000 cotton fabric squares and triangles have been cut and pieced together to make this handsome quilt, each block requiring seventy-three separate pieces.

The quilt is reminiscent of a style popular in the early part of the nineteenth century. Freedom quilts were made by friends and family for a young man to celebrate the event of reaching twenty-one years. The quilt was usually put away until his engagement, at which time it was presented to his future bride.

Previous page: *Tumbling Blocks*, American, nineteenth century.

Log Cabin,
Pineapple Variation

c. 1870

Kentucky, USA

70 x 70 in. (178 x 178 cm)

PRIVATE COLLECTION

 The Log Cabin as a quilt pattern name is mentioned in the literature of the 1860s, and may have been inspired by Abraham Lincoln's presidential campaign of 1862. The Pineapple variation of the Log Cabin design is an extremely complicated pattern. The juxtaposition of light and dark shapes in this challenging quilt moves your eye through a series of changing patterns from four-pointed stars, to interlocking circles, bull's-eyes, and windmill sails. Made from lengths of old woolen cloth, this mesmerizing quilt is an outstanding example of the design inventiveness of quilters.

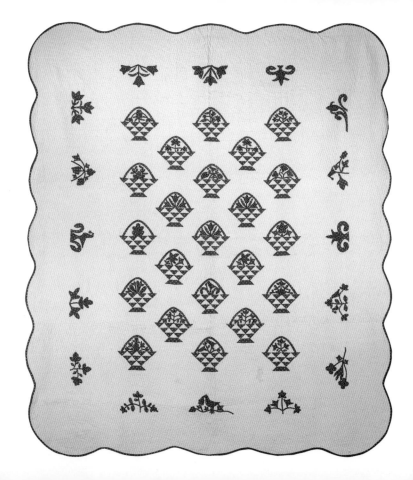

Birds in Baskets

1870

Pennsylvania, USA

90 x 80 in. (228.6 x 203.2 cm)

PRIVATE COLLECTION

The theme of birds and baskets, both of which appear in Colonial American chintz, *broderie perse*, and medallion quilts as early as the mid-eighteenth century, have been delightfully interpreted in this unusual and delicate quilt.

Spools

c. 1890
Kansas, USA
60 x 74 in. (152 x 188 cm)
PRIVATE COLLECTION

 Spools is a popular nineteenth-century scrap pattern and its name must lie close to the heart of any active needleperson. It would have taken the maker a long time to accumulate enough fabric remnants to make up the 2300 pieces needed for this quilt.

Quiltmakers spend many years collecting fabric scraps and in the nineteenth century when women of every age, class, and race sewed, scrap bags would have been common to all households. In it went leftover dress and furnishing fabrics as well as worn garments. Women exchanged their scraps and passed on their valuable collection to their children and grandchildren.

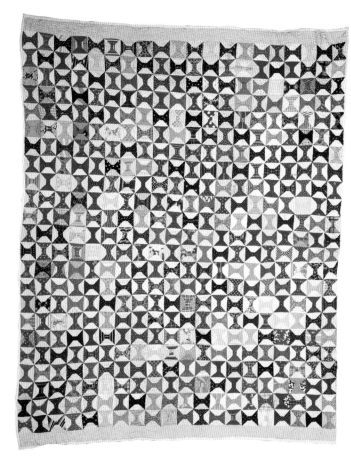

Pennsylvania Dutch Folk Art Appliqué

c. 1860
Pennsylvania, USA
72 x 92 in. (183 x 233 cm)
PRIVATE COLLECTION

 Pennsylvania Dutch quilts are filled with joyful folk images and motifs, recalling memories of the new settlers' German-speaking home. Worked in lively colors of red, green, and yellow with abundant patches of brightly patterned calico, these quilts are a sign of the optimism that abounded among these settlers.

This mid-nineteenth-century quilt, incorporating appliqué, piecing, reverse appliqué, and embroidered cording on a green background, has the decorative qualities of the gingerbread house found by Hansel and Gretel. The oak leaf is the main motif, worked around the border and in the body of the quilt, evoking a picture of an ancient oak wood.

Military Patchwork

c. 1870
England
72 x 76 in. (182 x 193 cm)

Generally speaking, quiltmaking has been, and continues to be, a female activity. Men may have assisted in the art—by cutting fabric or designing andbuilding quilting frames—but they have rarely participated in the actual piecing or quilting. From the large numbers of similar patchwork quilts made by the soldiers exhibited for the 1890 Royal Military Exhibition at the Chelsea Hospial in London, it can be safely assumed that this amazing mosaic quilt was worked by a man. Thousands of half-inch (1 cm) woolen squares, cut from regimental uniforms, have been pieced together in a variety of configurations to make up the twenty-five blocks. They are contained within a frame of smaller squares, finished with a zigzag border.

Mammy Quilt

signed and dated Lola 1902
USA
86 x 72 in. (218 x 193 cm)
PRIVATE COLLECTION

 The mammy quilt was an unusual twentieth-century quilting phenomenon in which white needlewomen portrayed their perception of black characters. The prevailing attitude in the early part of the century was one of deep-seated racism, so it is not surprising that the characters portrayed were stereotypes, such as Aunt Jemima, Little Black Boy, Sugar Pie, and Brown Koko.

Doll-like figures, each with a different, colorful frock and turban, have been appliquéd by machine onto a ground of cinnamon pink. All look left, except the one in the bottom right-hand corner who alone looks right. The fabric for the frocks may have been cut from cotton dry-goods sacks, which were often packaged in cheap and cheerful printed cotton.

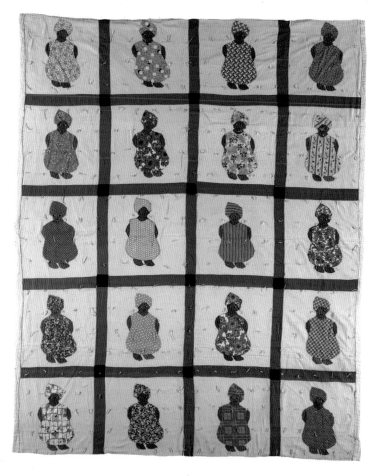

Grandmother's Flower Garden

made by Dena Williams
c. 1930
Wright City, Missouri, USA
72 x 96 in. (183 x 244 cm)
PRIVATE COLLECTION

Grandmother's Flower Garden, Dresden Plate, and Double Wedding Ring, were the most popular patterns of the early twentieth century.

Grandmother's Flower Garden is a one-patch design constructed from hexagon shapes, which emerge as a honeycomb when sewn together. Joining the hexagons into rings was a way of making the sewing more manageable. To create the garden, a mid-toned hexagon is used for the center. This is then surrounded by one or more rings of flower-colored prints, a ring of green for the foliage, and a ring of white to represent the path.

Log Cabin, Light and Dark Variation

c. 1880

Kentucky, USA

70 x 82 in. (178 x 208 cm)

PRIVATE COLLECTION

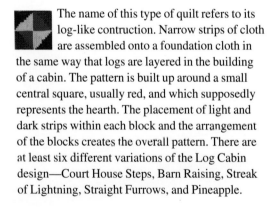 The name of this type of quilt refers to its log-like contruction. Narrow strips of cloth are assembled onto a foundation cloth in the same way that logs are layered in the building of a cabin. The pattern is built up around a small central square, usually red, and which supposedly represents the hearth. The placement of light and dark strips within each block and the arrangement of the blocks creates the overall pattern. There are at least six different variations of the Log Cabin design—Court House Steps, Barn Raising, Streak of Lightning, Straight Furrows, and Pineapple.

Primitive Schoolhouses

c. 1880
Vermont, USA
60 x 70 in. (152 x 178 cm)
PRIVATE COLLECTION

The one-room schoolhouse is a popular and symbolic motif in American culture. The quilt pattern was developed during the last half of the nineteenth century, and in the unsettled and dangerous world of the new frontier, it represented an achievement of stability and permanence for those that built and used it.

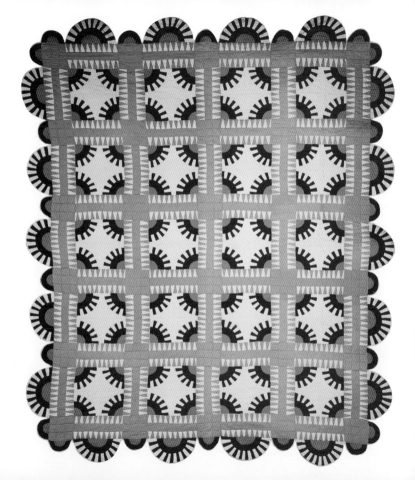

New York Beauty

c. 1920
Michigan, USA
96 x 80 in. (244 x 203 cm)
PRIVATE COLLECTION

Quilt pattern names are numerous and changeable, and frequently are influenced by the environment and circumstance of the maker. For instance, this pattern was known in the nineteenth century as Rocky Mountain Road and Crown of Thorns, reflecting a time when life was hard and hazardous for early settlers, and religion provided them a source of comfort. The name New York Beauty is resonant with the buoyancy of the twentieth century and the new and prosperous quilt industry.

This magnificent quilt dazzles the eye with vibrant color and remarkably accurate stitching. The sawtooth blocks, sashing, and circular appliqué combine to make this a technical masterpiece.

Yo-yo Quilt

1925
USA
62 x 84 in. (157.5 x 213.4 cm)
PRIVATE COLLECTION

 The Yo-yo quilt is a modern novelty quilt that emerged at the time of the yo-yo craze. It was particularly popular during the period 1925–1950 and was made as a decorative throw. It is not a quilt in the true sense of being made up of three layers and stitched together.

The yo-yo is made entirely of small circles of cloth about 3 inches (7.5 cm) in diameter, the edges are turned in and gathered with thread and fastened, so that the medallion is smooth on one side and puckered on the other. The separate medallions are joined either in a specific design or in a random way reminiscent of scrap quilts.

Evergreen

c. 1920
Texas, USA
66 x 86 in. (168 x 218 cm)
PRIVATE COLLECTION

 The tree, in all its varieties, has been a popular motif in American quiltmaking. This seasonal quilt, which expands our visual concept of Christmas, was made from a kit during the 1920s when commercially printed patterns encouraged quilters to embark on new and challenging projects. Commercial patterns meant that quilts were no longer exclusively one-of-a-kind, and they served to fuel a huge revival in quilting.

Victorian Crazy Crib Quilt

c. 1890
USA
18 x 24 in. (46 x 61 cm)
PRIVATE COLLECTION

 The crazy quilt was a curious invention of the Victorian period. Rather than geometric pieces of cotton calico, irregularly shaped scraps of velvet, brocade, and taffeta were used, often from worn-out garments and furnishing fabrics. They are frequently very personal keepsakes containing stitched moments of someone's life. The national passion for crazy quilts was shortlived, yet the stylistic concept continued well after the turn of the century using more ordinary fabrics, such as dark woolens and heavy suiting materials.

This piece is unusual because it features a central medallion of an embroidered bouquet of daisies surrounded by a traditional nine-patch block.

Princess Feather Variation

c. 1900
Skullkill County, Pennsylvania, USA
78 x 80 in. (198 x 203 cm)
PRIVATE COLLECTION

 The feather as an appliqué pattern probably evolved around the nineteenth century, and drew its inspiration from the feather quilting pattern. As a quilting pattern the feather motif dates back to the seventeenth century and there are many examples of it used in garments and coverlets.

The Princess Feather, of which there are many variations, is a large pattern demanding a lot of room. This version, worked in indigo blue and Turkey red on a white ground, is composed of just four blocks. The slightly mismatched and irregularly-shaped feathers, stars, and tulips appear to have been cut without a template. In contrast, the quilt has been very evenly stitched in a precise cross-hatching pattern.

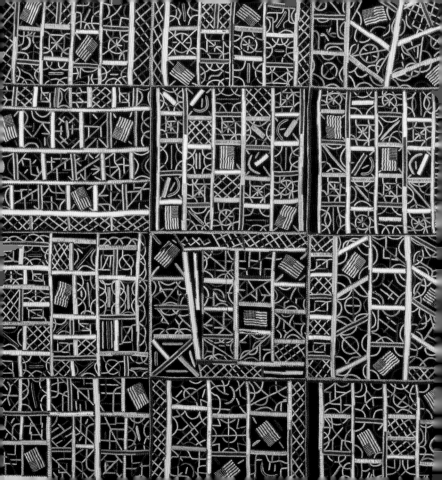

Patriotic Crazy Quilt

twentieth century

USA

68 x 56 in. (172 x 142 cm)

PRIVATE COLLECTION

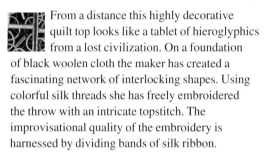 From a distance this highly decorative quilt top looks like a tablet of hieroglyphics from a lost civilization. On a foundation of black woolen cloth the maker has created a fascinating network of interlocking shapes. Using colorful silk threads she has freely embroidered the throw with an intricate topstitch. The improvisational quality of the embroidery is harnessed by dividing bands of silk ribbon.

Crazy work was not exclusively the domain of quilts. The delicacy of these pieces made them more suitable as decorative throws, screens, curtains, tea cosies, and mantlepiece scarves.

Whig's Defeat

c. 1860
Georgia, USA
90 x 93 in. (229 x 236 cm)
COURTESY VICTORIA WEIL

 Quilt pattern names can provide us with an interesting record of public interest and feelings on any number of issues.

From the political dispute during the 1840s between the Whigs and the Democrats, two new quilt patterns emerged—the Whig Rose and the Democrat Rose, with each party claiming their own. The dispute was resolved at the 1844 elections with the defeat of the Whig presidential candidate, Henry Clay, by the Democrat, James K. Polk. And from his demise sprang a new pattern name—Whig's Defeat.

Ohio Star

c. 1840
USA
76 x 90 in. (193 x 229 cm)
PRIVATE COLLECTION

This stunning quilt, with its exciting combination of a rare copper-plate Regency pillar print in the border, and plain blocks and Provençal inspired prints used to piece the Ohio star blocks, is a textile enthusiast's dream. Regency fabrics were strongly influenced by classical themes, hence the penchant for Greek and Roman columns.

The star is one of the oldest and most popular quilt motifs and at least a hundred variations can be identified.

Mennonite Baskets

c. 1880

Bloserville, Pennsylvania, USA
66 x 80 in. (167.6 x 203.2 cm)
PRIVATE COLLECTION

 This stylish and very modern looking quilt, signed S.K. and made at Waldo Berry Farm by Berry's grandmother, was given to her daughter Caroline. The Turkey red and chrome orange color combination was popular with quilters during the last years of the nineteenth century in Pennsylvania.

The Mennonites, like the Amish, are a cohesive Anabaptist sect who practice a lifestyle of simplicity and plain living. Originally from Switzerland, the Mennonites emigrated to Germany and later America at the invitation of William Penn.

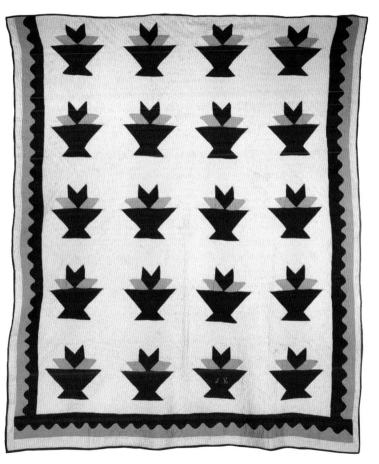

Amish Unknown Design

c. 1920

Mifflin County, Pennsylvania, USA

67 x 72 in. (170 x 183 cm)

PRIVATE COLLECTION

 This stunning quilt was made by members of the Nebraska Church, one of the strictest Amish orders, out of old buggy shawls. The Amish, to this day, use horsedriven buggies and are forbidden to use cars. Suggestive of a modern abstract landscape, perhaps a Paul Klee painting, this piece is a remarkable and unique expression of color and texture.

Rayed Star

c. 1900
USA
82 x 83¹⁄₂ in. (208.3 x 212 cm)
PRIVATE COLLECTION

 This 1900s, well-ordered Mennonite quilt boasts elaborate feather quilting around a pieced design of deceptively simple triangles. The strong sense of symmetry is charmingly offset by a wide scalloped border. The quilt is made up of equilateral triangle shaped blocks, which are tessellated to form the geometric pattern.

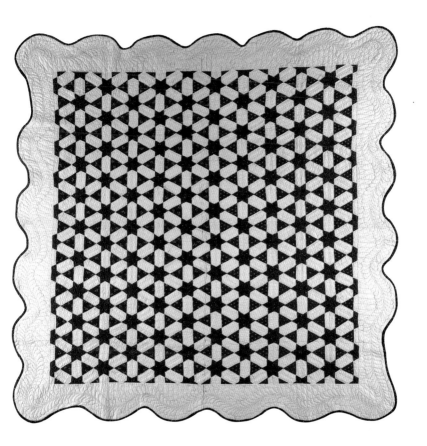

Feathered Star in
Blue and Gold

c. 1920
Kentucky, USA
76 x 78 in. (193 x 198 cm)
PRIVATE COLLECTION

 A variation of the basic eight-point star design, the feathered star motif is one of the intricate patchwork designs developed in the mid-nineteenth century. Its very complexity assigned it showpiece status, as a quilt brought out for special occasions.

This example in Wedgwood blue has been finished with a delicate sawtooth border that imitates the feathering of the internal blocks.

16-Patch on Point

c. 1860
Ohio, USA
90 x 96 in. (229 x 244 cm)
PRIVATE COLLECTION

Interesting printed calicos, triple row quilting, and blocks set on point transform this otherwise simple pattern into a noteworthy quilt. Although it is often hard to discern regional styles, recent state quilt projects have unearthed new information which help to characterize particular trends. Setting blocks on point, and diagonal rows of triple quilting are distinctive techniques discovered to have been popular with early Ohio quiltmakers.

North Carolina Lily

c. 1930
Missouri, USA
78 x 90 in. (198 x 203 cm)
PRIVATE COLLECTION

 One of the best loved and most handsome patterns based on the lily, this pattern is often composed using a diamond-shaped block. It was an extremely popular design that migrated across the continent bearing a variety of names to suit new locales. Names included Wood Lily, Mountain Lily, Fire Lily, and Meadow Lily, among others. This charming example features an unusual appliqué vine border.

Cherry Basket

c. 1930
USA
70 x 84 in. (178 x 213.4 cm)
PRIVATE COLLECTION

This colorful 1930s quilt is an exuberant example of a well-loved pattern. The slightly tipsy baskets have been pieced and then appliquéd onto a whole piece of fabric, creating a sense of warmth and spontaneity. The bright calico prints are typical of those popular during this period.

Amish Bars

c. 1930
Lancaster County, Pennsylvania, USA
70 x 80 in. (179 x 203 cm)
PRIVATE COLLECTION

A traditional pattern in colors much favored by Lancaster County Amish quilters, this stunning quilt could pass for a work of twentieth-century art. The simple geometric design was used by early Amish quilters in a conscious effort to avoid emulating the decorative and pictorial quilts made by the majority of American women in the 1870s. The stark linear motif has been complemented by a fabulously intricate quilting pattern featuring wreaths and climbing vines.

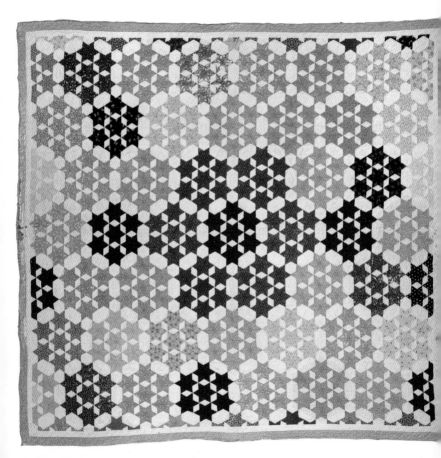

Seven Sisters

c. 1840
New England, USA
78 x 80 in. (198 x 203 cm)
PRIVATE COLLECTION

 This unusual early quilt, with its considered sense of symmetry and color, and wonderful collection of early fabrics, was rescued from the back seat of an old Chevy in St Louis. The design, which is rarely seen, takes its name from the Pleiades constellation of stars.

Love and Luck

c. 1900
Vermont, USA
70 x 80 in. (178 x 203 cm)
PRIVATE COLLECTION

 This exuberant quilt in patriotic colors of red, blue, and white was made using the paper-cutting method, popular among Pennsylvanian German communities.

The fabric is folded to precise specifications and then cut so that a perfectly symmetrical pattern is formed. Using the heart as a single motif, the maker has cleverly arranged it to create a clover shape, no doubt following the old adage of where there is love there is luck. A careful and simple symmetry is achieved in the design by setting the large clover motif on point and surrounding it by smaller versions in a square formation.

Bear's Paw

c. 1880
USA
54 x 72 in. (137 x 183 cm)
PRIVATE COLLECTION

 The Bear's Paw is one of those well-loved patterns which both typified and celebrated the romance of rural life. This example, from the midwest, is well-balanced and harmonious in the overall scale of design and color combinations.

Bear's Paw is the traditional name for several patterns in western Pennsylvania and Ohio, where bear tracks were a common sight. The same basic pattern also goes by the names Duck's Foot in the Mud, Hands of Friendship, and Hands All Around.

Carpenter's Square

late nineteenth century

USA

60 x 75 in. (151.8 x 191.1 cm)

PRIVATE COLLECTION

 Sources of inspiration for many quilts can be either domestic objects like cake stands and baskets, or natural elements like flowers and birds. It is unusual to find a quilt which is directly named after a household tool.

Another interesting feature of this late-nineteenth-century quilt is the curved machine quilting, a point which testifies to the growing pride which accompanied the ownership of a sewing machine.

Red and Green
Floral Appliqué

c. 1850
Pennsylvania, USA
86 x 86 in. (218 x 218 cm)
PRIVATE COLLECTION

 This cheerful red and green appliqué quilt was made before the American Civil War. The maker has used symbolic motifs that express permanence, freedom, and well-being—schoolhouses flanked by the great Charter Oak create a border around the bountiful harvest wreaths. The one-room schoolhouse is a significant American symbol. In the primitive and often dangerous New World, it came to represent stability and respectability.

Legend has it that when James II of England demanded the surrender of the Colonial Charter of Connecticut to the Dominion of New England, it was hidden in the Charter Oak of Hartford, Connecticut.

Mennonite Starburst

c. 1920
Pennsylvania, USA
84 in x 84 in. (213.4 x 213.4 cm)
PRIVATE COLLECTION

 A unique application of the star motif, this inspired Mennonite quilt has elaborate patterns of feather, scroll, and wreath quilting on the solid blue background. The central pieced star is reminiscent of German motifs often found painted on Pennsylvania barns.

String of Flags

late nineteenth century
USA
72 x 88 in. (182.9 x 223.5 cm)
PRIVATE COLLECTION

 Made entirely of what appears to be patterned shirting material, this deceptively simple quilt is a pleasant variation on the ever-present triangle. The muted tonality of the quilt gives it both a homey and a sophisticated appearance.

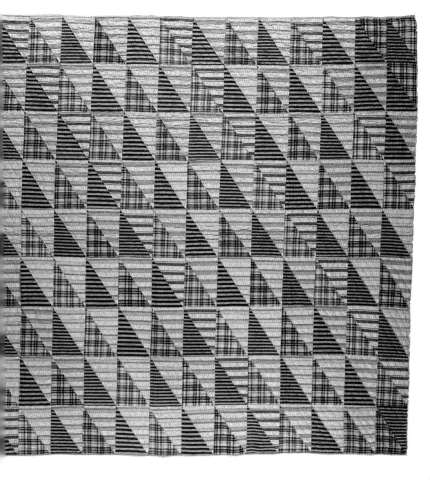

Pyramids

c. 1900
USA
51 x 86 in. (129.5 x 218.4 cm)
PRIVATE COLLECTION

 This simple design is created by sewing bands of alternating colored and plain triangles. The name Pyramids refers to the triangle shape used: a short baseline triangle. In this quilt of lush Victorian velvets, the black triangles vie for dominance with identically sized triangles pieced from narrow colorful strips. When the quilt is viewed vertically, the pattern appears as a zigzag basket weave. In a horizontal position, the black faced triangles appear three-dimensional, with the colored triangles providing the illusion of depth.

Alphabet Quilt

c. 1930
USA
70 x 90 in. (178 x 229 cm)
PRIVATE COLLECTION

 Commercial pattern houses made a significant contribution to the twentieth-century quilt revival. The wealth of attractive new patterns and their easy availability through magazines, newspapers, and mail order houses inspired many women to make quilts. The Nancy Page Quilt Club with the Publishers Syndicate, New York, offered patterns for alphabet blocks weekly through the newspapers.

This highly amusing and individual alphabet quilt has only fifteen letters and the peculiar choice of words suggests that the maker was engaged in some game or wordplay with the three boys for whom it was made—Bruce, David, and Steven, whose names are stitched on this quilt.

Maple Leaf

c. 1880

Holmes County, Ohio, USA

66 x 72 in. (167.6 x 182.9 cm)

PRIVATE COLLECTION

 It is hard to imagine that this strikingly modern looking quilt was made by a Holmes County housewife around 1880. Chrome orange and Turkey red was a popular color combination during this period.

Zigzag Bricks

c. 1880
Missouri, USA
67 x 83 in. (171.5 x 212 cm)
PRIVATE COLLECTION

Made in Missouri around 1880, this
simple yet striking quilt displays a
fascinating array of the small-scale and
soberly colored prints that were fashionable during
the latter part of the nineteenth century.

Prairie Stars with Prairie Points

1880

Mid-West, USA

66 x 84 in. (167.6 x 213.4 cm)

PRIVATE COLLECTION

This quilt consists of Turkey red stars on a white background. It is an interesting variation with pieced eight-point stars in the corners of each star block. A decorative border of folded prairie points complements the fascinating graphic design.

Spring Bouquet

1930

USA

88 x 104 in. (223.5 x 264.2 cm)

PRIVATE COLLECTION

 Of the thousands of quilt patterns which were published in the USA in the 1930s, this appealing floral appliqué uses pastel shades which were fashionable between the wars.

Dresden Plate

1930
St Louis, Missouri, USA
90 x 106 in. (228.6 x 269.2 cm)
PRIVATE COLLECTION

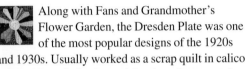 Along with Fans and Grandmother's Flower Garden, the Dresden Plate was one of the most popular designs of the 1920s and 1930s. Usually worked as a scrap quilt in calico prints, this variation is a celebration of rayon and acetate satin. Designed as a cheap substitute for silk that came into commercial use at the turn of the century, rayon enjoyed a short-lived popularity for making crazy quilts, coverlets, comforters, and cushion covers.

Amish Lone Star

c. 1920
Texas, USA
82 x 88 in. (208.3 x 223.5 cm)
PRIVATE COLLECTION

Variously known as Star of Bethlehem and Star of the East, star quilts of this sort were generally brought out for Christmas. This mesmerizing example is pieced point by point. Forty-eight diamonds of equal size are arranged in rows of different lengths to form the eight diamond-shaped points. The star is asymmetrically placed, allowing for an exceptionally beautiful detailed pillow panel. The coverlet is finished with the distinctive triangle and scallop edge border, a technique popular between 1925 and 1950.

Double Irish Chain

c. 1880
Delaware County, Pennsylvania, USA
84 x 90 in. (213.4 x 228.5 cm)
PRIVATE COLLECTION

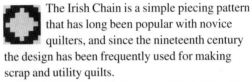

The Irish Chain is a simple piecing pattern that has long been popular with novice quilters, and since the nineteenth century the design has been frequently used for making scrap and utility quilts.

This quilt is pieced in Turkey red (a fashionable natural red dye of the period), green, and cream, and has been beautifully quilted and finished with an elegant border.

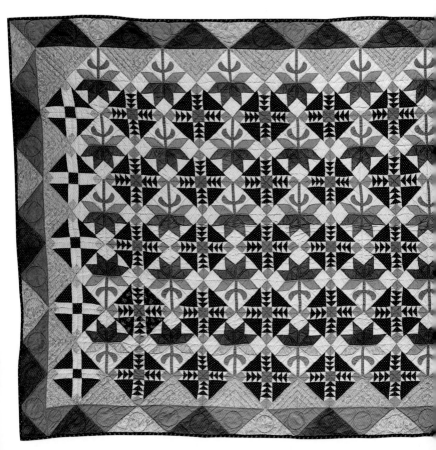

Missouri Folk Art Lily

1850s
Missouri, USA
64 x 82 in. (162.5 x 208.3 cm)
PRIVATE COLLECTION

 This is a unique design and reveals the
high level of design sophistication
achieved by many nineteenth-century
quiltmakers. The complicated piecing
arrangement of small interlocking triangles is
testimony to the extraordinary technical skill of
the maker.

Cake Stand

1890s
USA
68¼ x 74½ in. (173.4 x 189 cm)
PRIVATE COLLECTION

This striking 1890s quilt has a real patchwork feel, while the design is inspired by an important domestic accessory. The intricate piecework and attention paid to scale, direction, and proportion, are effectively presented through a highly contrasting color scheme. The design is intensified by the series of alternating color borders and binding.

Iris

1930s
USA
96 x 78 in. (244 x 198 cm)
PRIVATE COLLECTION

 The six-sided, lozenge-shaped background of each block of the quilt creates a compelling setting for these colorful irises. Although the designer, Ruby Short McKim, provided instructions for this design, it was the maker's personal interpretation to add the charming inner green border that gracefully follows the block contour. The design is further individualized by the decorative top-stitching on the Deco-inspired petals and stems.

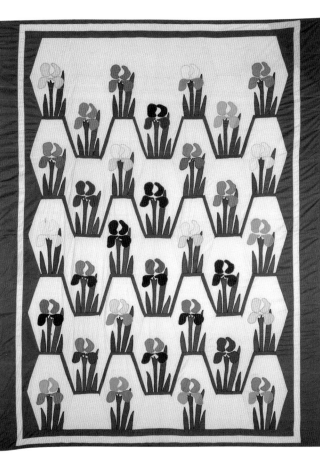

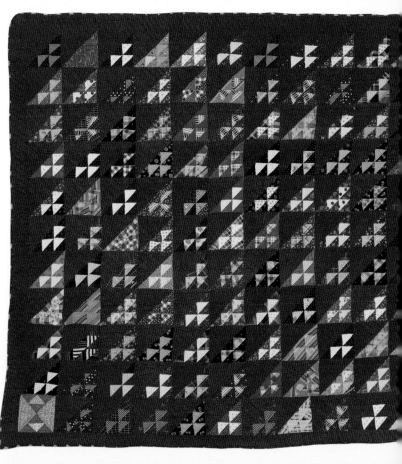

Birds in the Air

c. 1890
North Carolina, USA
72 x 84 in. (182.9 x 213.4 cm)
PRIVATE COLLECTION

The light triangles which seem to flutter across the surface of this quilt are evocative of the flight of birds on their autumn migration—hence the name of this traditional patchwork pattern, Birds in the Air. It was made around 1890 in North Carolina and displays some of the characteristics of a traditional Appalachian quilt: a dark background fabric with rather large quilting stitches.

175

Early Nine-patch

early 1800s
USA
92 x 102 in. (234 x 259 cm)
PRIVATE COLLECTION

 The nine-patch design is a simple pattern, popular with novice and experienced quilters alike. It is a good design for the novice because it is simple to cut and piece, and for the experienced quilter, it provides the basis of many more difficult patterns.

Thistle Appliqué

1860
Pennsylvania, USA
80 x 92 in. (203.2 x 233.7 cm)
PRIVATE COLLECTION

This charming piece is typical of the American penchant for red, white, and green quilts, a style favored by German immigrants in Pennsylvania. Appliqué patterns from the middle of the last century often featured swag borders and a variety of bows, hearts, and flower motifs. The generous dimensions of this quilt reflect the use of large family beds which were in vogue prior to the American Civil War in 1862.

Mennonite Log Cabin, Barn Raising Variation

c. 1910
Quakertown, Pennsylvania, USA
75 x 75 in. (190.5 x 190.5 cm)
PRIVATE COLLECTION

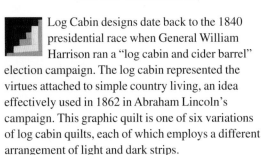 Log Cabin designs date back to the 1840 presidential race when General William Harrison ran a "log cabin and cider barrel" election campaign. The log cabin represented the virtues attached to simple country living, an idea effectively used in 1862 in Abraham Lincoln's campaign. This graphic quilt is one of six variations of log cabin quilts, each of which employs a different arrangement of light and dark strips.

Basket with Eight-point Star

c. 1890
USA
66 x 80 in. (167.6 x 203.2 cm)
PRIVATE COLLECTION

 Baskets have always been a popular folk art motif. This charming quilt uses a symmetrical combination of both baskets and stars, making it a romantic interpretation of a traditional pattern.

The idea of art became a popular notion around this time and the widespread public confirmation of the moral value in art and design had two important effects on quilting. Firstly, it helped to reaffirm the woman's belief in her own creative handiwork. Secondly, the romanticism which permeated American culture encouraged the continuation of traditional quilting techniques which existed alongside newer methods.

Bluebird

1952

Tennessee, USA

83 x 83 in. (210.8 x 210.8 cm)

PRIVATE COLLECTION

 Made in Tennessee in 1952, this delightful quilt has the innocence and charm of a rustic quilt. The large template pieces and smooth curves make this a simple design to appliqué.

Log Cabin, Hap Quilt

1880s
Pennsylvania, USA
78 x 76 in. (198 x 193 cm)
COURTESY GIDEON WEIL

This rugged-looking Log Cabin style quilt has been made using a variety of what appears to be scraps of suiting material and woolen fabrics. A Hap quilt is commonly known as a comforter.

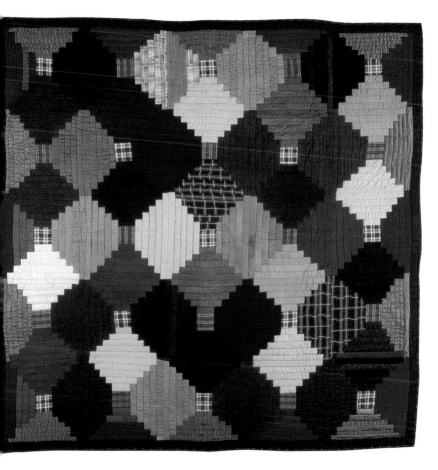

Album Quilt

1862
Pennington, New Jersey, USA
80 x 90 in. (203 x 228.6 cm)
PRIVATE COLLECTION

This remarkable quilt was made by members of the Ketcham family. Each block of the quilt is composed of different motifs, and several are inscribed in indelible ink with poems, sayings, and biblical references. The fabrics used are a combination of fine chintzes and glazed and plain cottons, often featuring intricate trapunto quilting. This stunning work testifies to the national penchant for documenting in quilts the close bonds that exisited among families and communities during the nineteenth century.

Amish Diamond in a Square

c. 1930
Lancaster County, Pennsylvania, USA
78 x 78 in. (198 x 198 cm)
PRIVATE COLLECTION

This abstract, geometric design with dramatic use of vivid and saturated color is the hallmark of modern art and a modern lifestyle. The same words aptly describe this typical Amish quilt, yet it was made by a community that shuns a modern lifestyle.

The Diamond in a Square is a popular Amish design—a square within a square. It is a development of the central medallion style of quilt, and its design simplicity illustrates the Amish pursuit of spiritual truth through a philosophy of simplicity. This fine wool quilt is a wonderful example of the awe-inspiring color preferences of the Amish quilters in Pennsylvania.

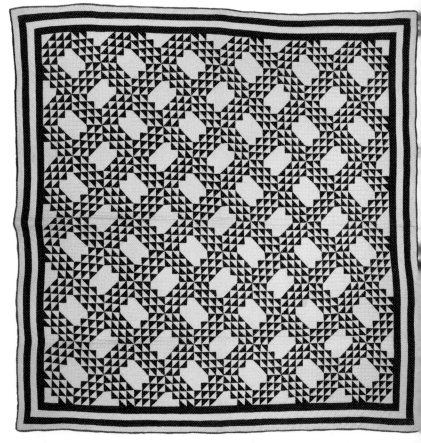

Ocean Waves

c. 1880
Ohio, USA
68 x 72 in. (173 x 183 cm)
PRIVATE COLLECTION

 Throughout the nineteenth century, indigo-dyed blue and white was a popular color choice for both pieced and appliqué quilts, as well as woven coverlets.

Indigo was introduced to Europe from India in the mid-sixteenth century, and replaced the extremely difficult blue-dye technique using plant woad. It remained in use as the main source of blue dye until 1856 when synthetic aniline dyes were invented.

This quilt is a challenging piecing exercise, and is a testimonial to the maker's sewing ability; several thousand, tiny one-inch (2.5-cm) triangles have been sewn together to create the dark grid that represents the ocean waves.

Rose Wreath

c. 1881
USA
78 x 96 in. (198.1 x 243.8 cm)
PRIVATE COLLECTION

The delicate quilting of an all-over heart pattern suggests that this colorful bedcover may have been made to celebrate a wedding. It has been expertly appliquéd with motifs in bright shades of red and blue with chrome orange accents that are cleverly echoed in the decorative border.

Stars

1855
Texas, USA
88 x 94 in. (223 x 238 cm)
PRIVATE COLLECTION

 The star pattern has been used repeatedly throughout the history of quiltmaking, and the possible variations are seemingly endless. It is very popular, and is used more than any other pattern in quiltmaking.

As well as representing a hopeful and romantic image, the star pattern also offers a needlework challenge. Most star patterns are constructed from diamond-shaped pieces. Cutting and sewing these acute angles with precision requires great skill. Like a jigsaw puzzle, all the pieces must fit precisely together, as any variation will throw the whole pattern out. Countless Lone Star quilt tops exist unfinished because of an error in the piecing.

Underground Railroad

c. 1870

USA

90 x 90 in. (229 x 229 cm)

PRIVATE COLLECTION

The resonance of the bitter debate on slavery is felt in the naming of this quilt. The underground railway was an organization of individuals who helped spirit slaves away to safety in the North and Canada.

This two-color quilt is a simple nine-patch construction of thirty-six blocks. However, the finished appearance is one of considerable complexity. The strong diagonal thrust dominates its square construction and requires the viewer's concentration to see the nine-patch block.

Cowboy Quilt

c. 1940s
USA
86 x 66 in. (218.4 x 167.6 cm)
COURTESY GIDEON WEIL

 Possibly derived from a 1940s quilt kit, this design has been painstakingly personalized with detailed and elaborate embroidery. Distinctive quilting radiates in a sunburst pattern from the center, and there is a fine feathered border around the beautifully scalloped edge. The rather inspired central motif bears a strong resemblance to earlier central medallion styles, the colors of the appliquéd figures having been carefully chosen to give a three-dimensional quality to the scene.

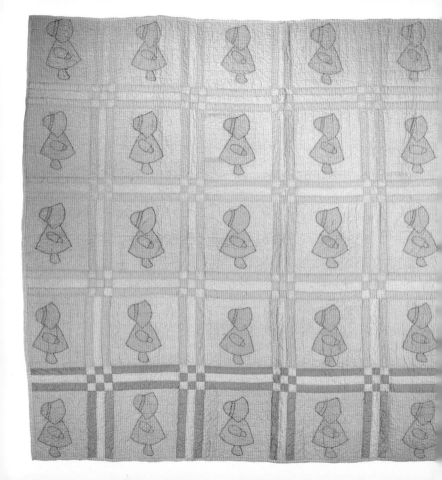

Sunbonnet Sue

1930
Missouri, USA
68 x 84 in. (172.7 x 213.4 cm)
PRIVATE COLLECTION

A nostalgic design popularized in the 1930s, this is one of the thousands of patterns that was commercially distributed throughout the United States. The silhouetted image of Sue bears a remarkable similarity to early Kate Greenaway drawings and Dutch engravings. The sentimental motif may have been appropriated by twentieth-century quilters to satisfy a longing for simplicity and a return to traditional rural values.

Amish Crown of Thorns

c. 1920
Iowa, USA
72 x 72 in. (183 x 183 cm)
PRIVATE COLLECTION

Although deeply devout, the Amish quilter used few patterns with an obvious religious connection. The Crown of Thorns is a rare exception to this rule. Many Amish quilt patterns may have specific pictorial names, but they are pieced using abstract geometric shapes, because pictorial realism in a quilt top is forbidden by the Amish Church. This pattern is a simple construction which artfully employs triangles and squares.

Summer Berries

1860
Pennsylvania, USA
74 x 80 in. (188 x 203.2 cm)
PRIVATE COLLECTION

 Floral appliqué quilts are usually valued for their realistic representation and their fine needlework. This cornucopia of summer berries sweeps into a secondary design of interlocking circles and four-pointed stars. Once the eye has established the circles, it is hard to read the quilt as clusters of berries. The strength of the geometric illusion has subdued the imagery to a secondary role.

The quilt has been beautifully appliquéd and the plump appearance of the berries has been achieved using a technique called trapunto. Also called Italian quilting, it is a method of quilting in which double rows of stitching form pockets, which are filled from the back of the quilt with cotton batting.

Mariner's Compass

c. 1860
New York State, USA
67 x 87 in. (170 x 221 cm)
PRIVATE COLLECTION

 A circle with radiating points is an old quilt pattern, and is thought to have evolved from the wind roses found on compass points and sea charts. The earliest known quilts bearing this pattern are English and date back to the eighteenth century.

This elegant variation has been worked in a distinguished palette of brown, red, pink, white, and green, using a lovely selection of nineteenth-century small print cotton fabrics. It is a challenging quilt design to construct because it requires extremely accurate cutting and piecing to ensure that the narrow and sharp points meet precisely.

Love Apple

c. 1870
Pennsylvania, USA
84 x 76 in. (213 x 193 cm)
PRIVATE COLLECTION

The love apple is more familiarly known as the tomato, which, at the time that this quilt was made, was prized by gardeners and considered to be an aphrodisiac. The regularly placed fruits on their vine are framed by an intricate chrome yellow, pink, and green diamond border.

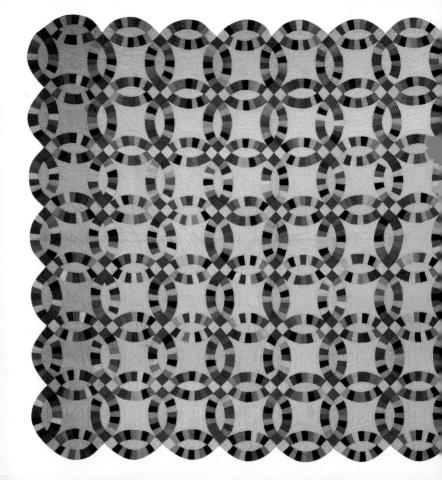

Double Wedding Ring

c. 1930
USA
72 x 82 in. (183 x 208 cm)
PRIVATE COLLECTION

This challenging pattern of interlocking rings, thought originally to have been a German design, came to symbolize the bands of marriage and was often given as a wedding gift. It was introduced in the mid-nineteenth century and reached its height of popularity in the early twentieth century with the advent of pre-cut templates, which made this exacting quilt pattern very much easier to make.

Amish Log Cabin, Barn Raising Variation

c. 1900
Pennsylvania, USA
76 x 80 in. (193 x 203 cm)
PRIVATE COLLECTION

Another popular design amongst Amish
quiltmakers is the Log Cabin, of which
there are many variations. The design is
made using light and dark colored strips sewn
around a central square. The placement of light
and dark strips dictates the resulting pattern.
For instance, by arranging the strips in diagonals
of light and dark, you can create the Barn Raising
and Straight Furrows patterns.

Centennial Eagle

c. 1876
Philadelphia, USA
70 x 88 in. (178 x 223 cm)
PRIVATE COLLECTION

The Centennial celebrations in America produced a burst of creative energy on all levels of art, craft, and needlework. Fabrics specially printed with flags, eagles, and other patriotic themes were manufactured for quiltmakers.

This quilt, appliquéd in red and green on a white ground, was made for the Exhibition. Its central motif is the Federal Eagle, flanked by two diminutive songbirds. Ten wheels with spokes of carnation stems surround the three birds. There is a refreshing lack of uniformity to the appliqué pieces. They have been cut without a template—each carnation stem is different from the next, the central rosettes are of varying shape and size, and the saw-tooth border is as unique as any mountain range.

Ohio Rose Appliqué

1930
USA
62 x 80 in. (157.5 x 203.2 cm)
PRIVATE COLLECTION

 Subtle shades of green and pink with pale yellow and bright red accents on a cream ground help bring this beautiful quilt to life. There is exceptionally fine echo quilting around the twelve appliqué blocks, and the surrounding vine border helps complete its charm.

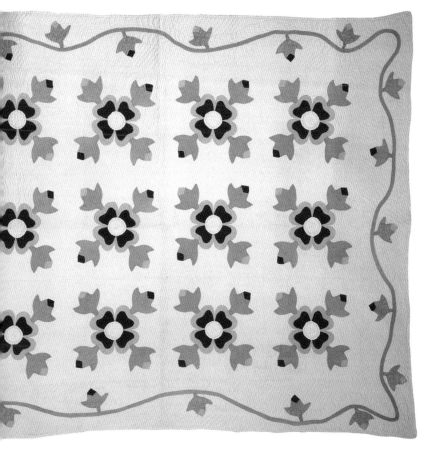

Tree of Life

c. 1911
Blue Ridge Mountains, North Carolina, USA
62 x 74 in. (157.5 x 188 cm)
PRIVATE COLLECTION

The tree is a popular motif in quiltmaking, and first appears on eighteenth-century chintz cut-out appliqué or *broderie perse* quilts. The decorative flowering tree offered a sense of domestic comfort in what was, for many, a great and frightening wilderness. By the nineteenth century settlers faced the natural world with confidence. They had domesticated the massive white pine that once filled their forefathers with awe and longing for the neat woods of Europe. It provided them with life-sustaining materials—timber for their log cabins and fuel for their fire, as well as furniture, cutlery, turpentine, paint, and tar.

Other variations on the triangular-shaped tree are Tree of Temptation, Temperance Tree, and Pine Tree.

Sailors

c. 1940

USA

84 x 66 in. (213 x 167 cm)

PRIVATE COLLECTION

 The twentieth century saw a proliferation of pieced and appliqué patterns inspired by everyday objects. While nineteenth-century quiltmakers abstracted reality into geometric patterns, the twentieth century sought a new realism in design. No object was too banal to immortalize in fabric—umbrellas, shoes, cups, cars, turtles, trolley cars, and donkeys all appeared on quilts. In the use and repetition of everyday objects, these light-hearted quilts can be seen as forerunners of the pop art movement.

Charles Lindbergh Commemorative Quilt

1930
USA
76 x 83 in. (193 x 211 cm)
PRIVATE COLLECTION

The rush of technological achievement in the twentieth century was cause for celebration, and from the excitement, a host of new quilt patterns emerged.

The solo flight of Charles Lindbergh across the Atlantic in the *Spirit of St Louis* airplane in 1927, caught the popular imagination, and commercial pattern makers were quick to produce this design.

Twenty-one single engine airplanes in white calico on a saffron yellow ground have been simply pieced and finished with an appliquéd propeller.

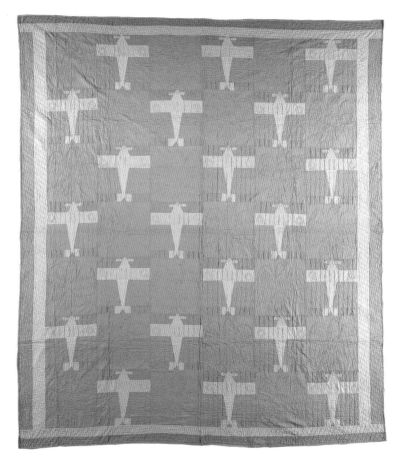

Shoo-fly

c. 1860
USA
72 x 72 in. (183 x 183 cm)
PRIVATE COLLECTION

"Flies in the buttermilk shoo, fly, shoo
Flies in the buttermilk shoo, fly, shoo
Flies in the buttermilk shoo, fly, shoo
Skip to my Lou my darling."

 This quilt teems with vitality—like a swarm of flies around the milk pot. The name is also associated with the famous Shoo-fly pie: a gooey, spiced cake baked with molasses in a flaky pastry, which being so sweet attracts flies during the baking.

The shoo-fly block is a simple nine-patch design, and in this variation the four corner blocks have been cut in half to make triangles. giving the block its busy appearance.

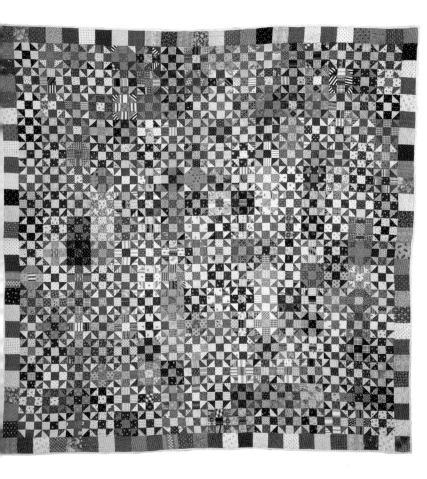

Coxcomb and Currant Variation

c. 1850
Peewee Valley, Kentucky, USA
75 x 80 in. (191 x 203 cm)
PRIVATE COLLECTION

 This exquisitely sewn, nineteenth-century quilt is a unique treatment of several very old piecing and appliqué patterns. The central intersecting pink and green cross is the Wild Goose Chase pattern. It is one of the earliest known patterns and dates back to the first half of the eighteenth century. The currants form a cruciform on top of the Wild Goose Chase and the showy coxcombs sweep across the composition like an oriental feathered fan.

The quilt has been executed in the favorite palette of nineteenth-century appliqué quiltmakers—red and green cottons with accents of bright pink and yellow, on a white background.

Flying Geese

c. 1880
USA
76 x 88 in. (193 x 224 cm)
PRIVATE COLLECTION

The traditional Flying Geese pattern assembled in neat rows creates an elegant contrast to the flowing vine border which has been worked with decorative trapunto leaves and berries. The fabrics chosen for the triangles represent a beautiful selection of nineteenth-century madder-style dyed prints.

Mennonite Joseph's Coat

c. 1920
Pennsylvania, USA
70 x 78 in. (178 x 198 cm)
PRIVATE COLLECTION

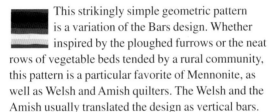 This strikingly simple geometric pattern is a variation of the Bars design. Whether inspired by the ploughed furrows or the neat rows of vegetable beds tended by a rural community, this pattern is a particular favorite of Mennonite, as well as Welsh and Amish quilters. The Welsh and the Amish usually translated the design as vertical bars.

Inspired by the Biblical story about Joseph and his coat of many colors, this quilt is a visual feast of color and quilting patterns. Pieced in narrow columns of plain cotton fabric, each of the seven different colored columns has been quilted with a different pattern—chains, diamonds, cable, zigzag, feather, and a meandering Greek pattern.

Churn Dash

1930
USA
60 x 82 in. (152.4 x 208.3 cm)
PRIVATE COLLECTION

Like its namesake, this unevenly pieced quilt has a very rustic charm about it. And on inspection of seams and quilting stitches, we can suppose that it may have been the maker's first attempt at making a quilt. This traditional pattern in period printed textiles is composed of twenty-four-pieced blocks separated by blue printed sashing.

Oakleaf and Reel Presentation Quilt

c. 1850
Pennsylvania, USA
101 x 101 in. (257 x 257 cm)
PRIVATE COLLECTION

This handsome quilt is an individual interpretation of the traditional Oakleaf and Reel pattern. It carries a personal inscription, beautifully written in indelible ink on the central block—"A Donation to the Rev John Farquhar from the Ladies of the Chanceford Congregation."

Amish Broken Star

1940s
Ohio, USA
76 x 76 in. (193 x 193 cm)
PRIVATE COLLECTION

 The star is one of the earliest and most enduring quilt motifs, and it has spawned countless variations. Stars are popular with Amish quilters as they are a celebration of the heavens and God's grandeur, as well as requiring excellent sewing skills, a feature that has distinguished the Amish community.

Union Army
Encircled Star

c.1860
USA
77 x 77 in. (195.6 x 195.6 cm)
PRIVATE COLLECTION

It is said that this unique and highly complicated design quilt was made at a quilting bee for a fundraising auction supporting the Union Army. Pieced in the strong union colors of navy-blue and Cheddar yellow, this quilt is a celebration of the imaginative sense of design and the extraordinary sewing skills that characterized much of nineteenth-century quilting in America.

Paradise Tree Appliqué

c.1930
Pennsylvania, USA
80 x 86 in. (203 x 218 cm)
PRIVATE COLLECTION

 This lovely delicately colored quilt recalls Elizabethan crewel embroidery and the central tree design is reminiscent of the colorful Indian printed cottons that frequently featured the Tree of Life motif. This pattern was issued as a quilt kit which would have supplied the maker with some or all of the required materials.

Silk Tumbling Blocks

c. 1870

USA

74 x 75 in. (188 x 191 cm)

PRIVATE COLLECTION

 Sketchy provenance on this quilt suggests that it was made out of ball gowns from a family in Louisville, Kentucky. It is a glorious array of patterned and plain silks and taffetas arranged to achieve the three-dimensional illusion.

The Victorians were fascinated by optical illusion and incorporated some of the principles into their quiltmaking. Depending on how you view this quilt, the blocks change from appearing as an opened concertina of postcards to blocks that seem to radiate from the center of the quilt. It is a one-patch design, formed from three diamond-shaped pieces, rather than from squares. The illusion is achieved by the placement of light, medium, and dark colors.

Rainbow Schoolhouses

c. 1940
USA
76 x 80 in. (193 x 203 cm)
PRIVATE COLLECTION

 The American one-room schoolhouse has long been a potent symbol of a community's stability and respectability, second only to the church. The schoolhouse pattern itself became a popular figurative motif at the end of the nineteenth century. This unusual example artfully employs rainbow-hued colors organized into diagonal bands, all of which are punctuated by bright pink stars.

Amish Nine-patch

c. 1920
Lancaster County, Pennsylvania, USA
81 x 82 in. (206 x 208 cm)
PRIVATE COLLECTION

This masterful nine-patch suggestively places solid black blocks within the central square, subtly echoing the Lancaster County fondness for the Diamond in the Square pattern.

In contrast to the geometric piecing the quilting is an intricate pattern of vines, wreaths, and clusters of grapes. The glowing quality of this piece may be attributed to the saturated color woolens as well as to a cloth used by the Amish of this period—Henrietta cloth—with its silk warp and wool weft.

Snow Crystals

c. 1920
Oklahoma, USA
71 x 90 in. (181.6 x 228.6 cm)
COURTESY VICTORIA WEIL

 Pattern names are often idiosyncratic and this one is perhaps no exception. This lovely quilt, made in Oklahoma during the 1920s, is a variation of the star design. The pattern was probably originally Arabic, and then spread to Europe and was adapted to Western culture. Blue and white have been the most popular quilt colors throughout the past century; this piece is particularly pleasing in that it subtly exploits two contrasting shades of blue. The twenty blocks are each given distinction by the darker blue sashing with center white posts.

Index